"JIFFY"

A Family Tradition

Mixing Business and Old-Fashioned Values

Cynthia Furlong Reynolds

THE ORIGINAL JIFFY MIX BOX AS INTRODUCED TO
THE PUBLIC IN APRIL 1930.

"JIFFY": A Family Tradition
Mixing Business and Old-Fashioned Values

Published by
Chelsea Milling Company
Chelsea, Michigan

Printed and bound in:
Grand Rapids, Michigan

Layout and design by
Diva Designs, Ann Arbor, Michigan

Library of Congress Control Number: 2008920710

ISBN 9780980232608

1 2 3 4 5 6 7 8 9 10

First Edition

www.jiffymix.com

CONTENTS

INTRODUCTION

The purpose of this story is to honor family–my family and my extended family, with many last names, who have worked at Chelsea Milling Company since it began in 1901. Together, the Holmes family and our family of employees have endured two world wars, the Great Depression, social unrest, personal tragedies, and revolutionary changes in the food industry. As a purely historical document, the story is interesting and engaging. But its true significance lies in its personal retelling of events shared by the many people who have shaped Chelsea Milling Company over the last 107 years.

As a fourth generation member of the Holmes family, the responsibility fell to me to make sure that these tribal stories were recorded before all of the storytellers were gone. Once the interviews for the book began, a true picture of the culture of Chelsea Milling began to develop.

I have always believed that the principles and values of any company will determine the effectiveness of the decisions it makes and the purity of the communication between its people. If the principles are sound and the values true, what results is a positive effect that gradually becomes visible in the overall behavior of a company. There is an old saying that goes to the core of any culture: "We judge ourselves by our intentions and we judge others by their behavior." If our intentions equal our behavior, we greatly increase the chance for true meaning.

We began the process for this book nearly eighteen years ago, in 1990. Mr. Joseph Clayton was chosen to conduct the interviews because of his experience doing historical research. He interviewed active employees as well as retirees and people who had business relationships with Chelsea Milling Company. Joe had gathered material from over twenty-five people when he unexpectedly passed away. I will never forget Joe's enthusiasm for this project. Several years went by and many storytellers were lost before the project found new life.

HOWARD "HOWDY" HOLMES, PRESIDENT AND CEO
OF THE CHELSEA MILLING COMPANY, WITH PHOTOS OF THE THREE GENERATIONS
OF HIS FAMILY WHO RAN THE MILL BEFORE HIM.

In 2001, two significant events took place that moved the book back to the forefront. My father, Howard Sumner Holmes, passed away and the book *Our Hometown: America's History as Seen Through the Eyes of a Midwestern Village*, about the history of Chelsea, Michigan, was published. We approached the author, Cynthia Furlong Reynolds, with the idea of completing our book. Cynthia picked up where Joe had left off and many more people were contacted and interviewed. With the passing of my father, many historical documents were also uncovered. Photos, letters, contracts, and journals were collected from his office and other storage areas previously untouched for decades. Through these precious documents, early life at the mill was revealed to us at last.

I want to thank the many people who have been a part of this effort: former employees, current employees, customers, and friends and family members. All have graciously contributed their time and memories to this project. However, one individual stands above all the rest.

Sandy Schultz started working at Chelsea Milling in 1984 as my father's assistant. Sandy adored Howard. For seventeen years she organized Dad's things and made sure he was comfortable. I have worked with Sandy since 1987, and I can say that without her devotion and loyalty this project would never have happened. Sandy is a lady who loves her work and puts her values first. As overseer of the company and family archives, she unearthed much of the history at the heart of this book. I am sure that without her enthusiasm and determination, and her loyalty to Chelsea Milling Company and the Holmes family, *"Jiffy": A Family Tradition* would never have been completed.

We hope you enjoy our story. I especially want to thank those who spent their entire working years at Chelsea Milling. As for the Holmes family, my direct family members who started and continued the mission, please know that although you may be gone, you will never be forgotten.

Howdy S. Holmes

Chelsea, Michigan
November 2007

"READY IN A JIFFY"

The Birth of America's First Prepared Baking Mix

The United States was about to enter the Great Depression—the worst financial crisis it had experienced—when Mabel Holmes pulled from the oven another experimental batch of freshly baked biscuits. Her husband, Howard S. Holmes, was hard at work trying to keep his business, the Chelsea Milling Company, afloat. Recently, he had been coming home with stories about friends, family members, and neighbors losing their jobs, their businesses, and their investments. Every day the newspapers and radios reported more bad news.

Fortunately, Mabel's family had fared better than most. The milling business had insulated them from the worst effects of the Depression. Mabel was both the daughter and the wife of a miller, a profession that was historically a position both of status and of service to the community. As a result, Mabel was well known and respected in Chelsea, Michigan, and also in the neighboring town of Ann Arbor, where she was an active member of numerous civic organizations. Each week the news she heard during her social outings was less encouraging, and she began to consider ways she and her family's milling business might help.

Great ideas can sometimes come from the most unexpected places. This time, the idea came from an incident that had occurred during the childhood of her twin boys, Dudley and Howard.

One morning they had brought a friend home to play. When noon arrived, Mabel had offered them lunch, but the young visitor had insisted on eating what his father had prepared and sent with him. Mabel couldn't help but notice the flat, unappetizing biscuits that the young boy's single father had attempted to make. She knew that light, flaky biscuits weren't easy to make, but these were exceptionally sad looking.

(LEFT) "THE MOST IMPORTANT ROOM IN A HOME MAY WELL BE THE KITCHEN," MABEL HOLMES ONCE TOLD A REPORTER. IN THE EARLY 1940S SHE DESIGNED HER OWN KITCHEN "TO AFFORD EVERY OPPORTUNITY FOR CONVENIENCE, COMFORT, AND CLEANLINESS." HER TWIN-OVEN STOVE HAD A ROTISSERIE AND A BROILER AND EVEN CAME EQUIPPED WITH A MANUALLY-OPERATED INCINERATOR.

And Mabel knew a good biscuit when she saw one. Being from a milling family, she had grown up in a home where baking was paramount. Her family had hired a black cook named Gulla whose biscuits were nothing short of legendary. Biscuits had been an important part of meals in those days, and they still were in the 1930s. But Mabel realized that not everyone had been raised with the luxury of an experienced cook or knew how to make melt-in-your-mouth biscuits themselves.

Inspired by that young boy's sad-looking biscuits, Mabel donned an apron, rolled up her sleeves, and set to work. She pulled out canisters of flour, sugar, baking powder, and baking soda, as well as milk and a pail of lard, and set to work experimenting. Her aim was to make a biscuit mix "so simple that even a man could do it."

No one knows how long it took her to determine the right ingredients and measurements. No one knows whether she began the project with her husband's approval or if she surprised him, but the result was a biscuit mix that was so easy, it only required adding milk to make perfect biscuits every time.

Howard S. Holmes was impressed with his wife's creation and they discussed developing it into a product that would be not only easy and convenient, but also affordable for families recovering from the recent economic downturn.

"First, we need a name," Mabel suggested.

It came to her one night when they were driving home from a Chicago business trip. Mabel remembered her childhood cook Gulla telling her, "Now, Miss Mabel, you go tell your father his good, hot biscuits will be ready in a jiffy."

"What do you think about the name JIFFY Biscuit Mix?" she asked Howard—and a good idea was about to become a reality.

Mabel went on to select the colors for the boxes that would introduce JIFFY to the public, and then she supervised the package design.

Seventy years later, Mabel's son Dudley described his mother as "brilliant, intuitive, and strong-minded, the kind of woman who nowadays would be the CEO of some big company."

But even the enterprising Mabel might not have foreseen the impact her creation would have on the nation. Introduced to the public in April 1930, Mabel's JIFFY Biscuit Mix launched America's package-mix industry and a new age of convenience.

Although Mabel was responsible for JIFFY's conception, JIFFY would never have reached the hands of American consumers without the Chelsea Milling Company and its four genera-tions of Holmes family ownership. But JIFFY's story begins even before the existence of the mill in its little Midwestern village of Chelsea. The story begins with the milling industry itself —and the way of life that developed around it.

CHELSEA'S MILL GETS ROLLING
The Mill and Village are Established Against the Odds

STAR OF THE WEST ROLLER MILLS WAS FOUNDED IN FRANKENMUTH, MICHIGAN, IN 1870 AND CONTINUES TO PRODUCE FLOUR TODAY.

Millers like to argue that *theirs* is the oldest profession in the world—and their claim isn't far from the truth. Millers were often the first entrepreneurs in a community. Their mill produced food for farmers' families and their animals, but millers also bought, sold, and traded homegrown commodities. Mills were usually the first commercial building in a settlement, and their production of ground meal was essential to settlers. Towns developed and flourished around them. Mills also served as informal community centers, bringing farmers from remote locations together with each other and with townspeople. Politics, prices, the weather, and local gossip were grist for the mill just as much as the grains were.

UNLIKE THE CHELSEA MILL, THE ANN ARBOR
MILL (ABOVE) STOOD ON A RIVER AND WAS
POWERED BY WATER. THE FLOUR MILL IN
SALINE (RIGHT) PROSPERED IN THE LATE
NINETEENTH CENTURY.

When mills started developing in southern Michigan, they were primarily water or wind powered. The winds in Michigan were strong and constant, but water proved to be more reliable. That's why most mills and the villages that developed around them were located along rivers or other moving bodies of water.

The village of Chelsea, settled in 1834 by two brothers, Elisha and James Congdon, was an exception. At first glance, nothing indicated that the Congdons' 460-acre holding would be suitable for establishing a flourishing village. The soil on their parcel was rich and marshy enough for onion fields and sandy enough for finer wheat crops, but water, that essential element, was missing. No river, lake, or pond was available to power a mill that could saw logs for new homes or grind grain for food. It turns out that a burned railroad stop may have actually been responsible for the development of a town where the odds were against it.

An 1881 map of Chelsea
locates the mill adjacent
to the Michigan Central
Railroad tracks.

Railroad station stops were usually built on locations where settlements already existed. Four miles west of the Congdon brothers' holdings there was already a small settlement with a railroad stop called Davidson's Station. One night Davidson's Station mysteriously burned down. Shortly afterward, the Michigan Central Railroad accepted Elisha Congdon's offer to build its new railroad stop on their land. The village of Chelsea quickly developed around it.

Unfortunately, little remains to give much detail about early life in Chelsea. All of the town's records were destroyed in a fire in the 1870s. No sketches, photographs, records of business transactions, or written descriptions remain. But surviving records from other settlements indicate that in the 1830s not a single mill existed in Washtenaw County, where Chelsea is located.

Around 1874, a mill was built along the Michigan Central Railroad tracks on the same site where the Chelsea Milling Company would later be located. The Chelsea map of 1881 shows a mill occupying town lot

numbers 16 and 17 on the north side of the railroad tracks; an 1895 map shows a flour mill on lot 16 only.

"I assume that the earliest mill here in Chelsea was run either by wind or by horsepower because we have no rushing river or mill pond," said Dudley Holmes Sr. "By the time my family became involved, steam powered the mill."

By the end of the nineteenth century, between 1,000 and 1,500 mills of all types had been constructed in Michigan, most of them powered by water. The Huron River, which runs through the southern part of the state, was dotted along its entire length with mills built for making salt, cider, flax, plaster, linseed oil, barrel staves, bonemeal, wool, textiles, and mustard. But the mills that prospered and remained were the mills built for lumber and grains—wheat, oats, barley, rye, and corn—that would provide food and income for villagers and farmers.

The success of these grain mills relied heavily on the local farmers. During the nineteenth century, farming was a labor-intensive business that required all the help it could get. Farms of 120 acres or more required two or three farmhands throughout the year and every able-bodied worker who could be recruited for harvesting. Generations of Chelsea's schoolchildren worked in the nearby onion fields; picked, husked, and scraped ears of corn; raked hay; picked and shelled beans; and helped harvest and thresh grains. Schools would close at harvest time so that children could work in the fields, drive wagons, or help with the picking, scything, bundling, shelling, and threshing.

Stories of farm life came firsthand from present-day Chelsea residents. Those who were born or raised here had close ties to the land. Often three or even four generations of a family lived together on a farm. Sometimes grandparents would retire to the village, leaving their farm to younger generations. Many shopkeepers, lawyers, and businessmen in town had family members living and working on farms outside Chelsea.

"We raised cows for milk, sheep for wool, wheat for the mill, and vegetables. We also kept our horses there," recalled Dudley Holmes Sr. of life on his family's farm north of town.

The grain harvest was a community-wide project, with teams of farmers' horses pulling wagons, and hired hands moving from farm to farm to harvest the grain, stack the stalks, load the stalks onto wagons, unload the stalks at the separators, and then store the grains and straw in the barns. Villagers would bring their children to the farms on weekends during summers, and at harvest time to help with the chores. Huge, elaborate meals fed the workers and their families.

"While the men and boys worked in the fields, every housewife tried to outdo the others with the meals. They were like Christmas feasts," remembered June Floyd Robinson, Howard Sumner Holmes's secretary.

THE EARLIEST KNOWN PHOTOGRAPH OF CHELSEA'S FLOURING MILL, TAKEN BEFORE THE CONSTRUCTION OF GRAIN TOWERS. THIS BUILDING, WHICH STILL EXISTS WITHIN THE CHELSEA MILLING COMPLEX, WAS AMONG THE FIRST LOCAL STRUCTURES TO BE CONSTRUCTED WITH CEMENT.

The Noah family's farm was a prime example. Their cash crop was wheat, and it was sold to the Chelsea Milling Company at harvest time. For three days, Laurence Noah with his two sons, Lynwood and Duane, along with several neighbors, would work long hours to harvest the grain as soon as John Otto and his threshing machine arrived. As was tradition, Mrs. Noah and her daughter, Donna (now Donna Lane), would prepare the extravagant meals that accompanied harvest time. Once the grain was harvested, it was transported to the mill to be ground into flour.

"For most of the twentieth century we got our wheat from the back of our local farmers' wagons," Dudley Holmes Sr. recounted. "Our mill was quite active in working with farmers from a large area around. We had contacts with all the small and big crop growers surrounding Chelsea."

Donna Lane remembers seeing long lines of farmers' wagons stretching

far beyond her house on State Route 52, all waiting their turn to sell their wheat to the Chelsea Milling Company. "They would line their wagons up along this road," Lane recalled. "It was a social time, a fun time for everyone. The children used to beg to come with their fathers. They ran through the fields and played with other children while the farmers gathered and talked as they waited to have their wheat weighed. No one was in a hurry."

Chelsea old-timers remember a childhood spent playing with their future wives and husbands while their fathers and the millers negotiated the price of wheat. Others remember the jobs they held at the mill during their high school years or during lean times on the farm.

B y 1879, Chelsea had all the amenities of civilized life: two newspapers, several cigar shops, tailoring businesses, a hat shop, barbershops, saloons, mercantiles, blacksmith shops, cooperages, and one flouring mill. The *Chelsea Standard* and *Chelsea Herald* (and, later, the *Chelsea Standard-Herald)* faithfully—and, often, weekly—reported on prospects for the wheat crop, the size of wheat harvests, and the mill's business, using them as barometers of the general prosperity of the town. That July, the *Herald* reported:

The wheat crop this year will go a long way toward deciding the financial problem. After all, the money must come out of the ground.

When the wheat crops were good, so was the mill's business; when the crops were bad, all local businesses suffered. The profits reported by Michigan's mills in 1879 were less than they had been fifteen years earlier. Still, farmers and merchants tried to stay optimistic. In the fall of 1879, a sign of economic upturn encouraged the newspaper's editor:

Our streets were completely lined with wheat teams last Saturday. We counted more than 152. The amount of wheat sold was 4,600 bushels. How is that for business? Chelsea can beat any town in the State, of its size, for buying produce.

In an effort to help promote the milling industry and to establish unified ethical standards, the Millers' National Association was founded in 1873. The association was launched by fifty-two millers, almost half of them from Michigan. At that time, Michigan had 488 millers, many of whom also belonged to the Michigan State Millers' Association.

Promoting business was always a concern among Michigan State Millers' Association members, just as it was for Chelsea's businesspeople.

"All who lived here in the earlier years were deeply interested and dependent on local industry and business," Chelsea attorney and historian John Keusch explained. "Buying or doing business out of town was frowned on."

In 1879 the *Chelsea Standard* reported a rumor that Chelsea's gristmill was about to be sold—unless local residents would agree to support the local business rather than "hauling their grain all over the county in search of more favorable rates." The editor suggested, "If the inhabitants will only encourage 'home industry,' there will be no danger of losing the mill." The *Chelsea Herald* lamented the fact that some farmers compared prices between Chelsea's mill and its competitors, and then hauled their wheat to the mill with the best price.

On June 5, 1879, the *Chelsea Herald* announced that F. E. E. I. Hatch had sold one-half of the lot on block 16—"on which is erected the Chelsea steam flouring mill"—to Charles T. Rogers for the sum of $2,300. This formed a dual ownership of the mill by Rogers and Hatch.

Later that year Ohio native Leaman Sparks, an experienced miller, bought the Chelsea Steam Mills from Rogers and Hatch. Sparks refitted the mill, installing $3,000 worth of new machinery—"the latest and most improved," according to the *History of Washtenaw County* published in 1881.

In spite of these improvements, the Sparks mill quickly became outdated with the introduction of the first major innovation in milling in several thousand years. Steel rollers began replacing the runs of stone on stone. The new steel rollers produced a finer grind of flour and eliminated stone chips which almost inevitably came with stone-ground wheat. Michigan's millers could both increase their output and improve the quality of their flours.

   As mills became more technically advanced and their output
increased, the competition for locally grown grains became more intense.
Neighboring mills sometimes employed creative marketing in their efforts
to convince Chelsea farmers to take their grains to other mills outside of
town. Once, George Merkel, the proprietor of the flour mill in Jerusalem,
located several miles south of Chelsea, brought a gift of two sacks of A No.
1 flour to the editor of the *Chelsea Herald*. Appreciative of the gift, the editor
gave the Jerusalem mill the following plug in the paper: "The editor's lady
says it was the best that she has ever used in Chelsea."

PETRIES MILL AT BLIND LAKE, MICHIGAN, SERVED THE LOCAL COMMUNITY WITH SEASONAL MILLING.

Within two months, Leaman Sparks was ready to fight flour with flour. He responded with an advertisement for the Chelsea Steam Flour Mill, promising that the mill *"keeps constantly on hand A No. 1 Wheat Flour, Graham Flour, Buckwheat Flour . . . Custom Work a Specialty. Farmers, please take notice and bring in your grists. Satisfaction guaranteed."* There's no way of knowing if his advertisement kept farmers from straying to other mills, but Sparks did retain ownership of the mill for several more years before passing it to the next owners.

E ach year brought its challenges to the milling industry. Farmers were at the mercy of changing weather and fluctuating market prices. And if that wasn't enough, just taking the harvested wheat to the mill could be downright dangerous. Teams of horses often gave Chelsea's townspeople something to talk about when they "took a lively runaway."

In 1881, the newspaper editor was most concerned about the fate of the area's entire wheat crop. By May, he was giving his opinion of what farmers and local businessmen could expect:

> While riding through the country the other day we noticed the large fields of wheat that the farmers were plowing up and preparing to plant corn, when last fall they had fond expectations of 40 bushels of wheat per acre.

At midsummer the farmers—and, undoubtedly, Chelsea's businessmen—were all worried about their finances. Each year the quality of life continued to relate closely to the success or failure of the harvest. If the wheat crop was good, everyone was certain to prosper.

By 1890, the U.S. Census Bureau announced that agriculture was America's leading industry, employing almost half the working population. Times were finally starting to look up, but the good news was short-lived.

Shortly after that census was taken, the firm of Wood & Hoag purchased the Chelsea mill from Leaman Sparks. Lynwood Noah, a lifelong friend of the Holmes family, sheds some light on this brief period of the mill's ownership. "My great-uncle William Wood owned part of the Chelsea mill around 1890, when it was operated under the name of Wood and Hoag, but he lost his share of the business three short years later, during the Depression of 1893. The Depression hurt a lot of people in America."

After the financial crisis of Wood & Hoag, articles indicate that the mill returned to F. E. I. Hatch, the owner before Leaman Sparks. On December 5, 1896, Mr. Hatch was the sole proprietor when a fire

(RIGHT) MICHIGAN MILLS PRODUCED FLOUR THAT OFTEN CARRIED DIFFERENT LABELS. THESE WERE SOME OF THE BRANDS SOLD BY CHELSEA MILLING COMPANY.

5 LBS.
NET WHEN PACKED

CHELSEA MILLING CO.
Snow Queen
PASTRY FLOUR

CHELSEA, MICHIGAN.
REGISTERED IN THE PATENT OFFICE BY MICHIGAN MILLING CO., 1902.
MATURED-BLEACHED
WITH META-COLORA

10 Lbs. Net Weight
COURT HOUSE
ENRICHED
BLEACHED
ENRICHED FLOUR
CHELSEA MILLING CO.
CHELSEA, MICH.

12-80

5 Lbs. Net When Packed.
FA-REE FLUFF

Cake Flour
CHELSEA MILLING CO.
CHELSEA, - MICH.
MATURED-BLEACHED
WITH META-COLORA

5 Lbs. Net Weight
"JIFFY"
SELF RISING
BLEACHED
ENRICHED FLOUR
CONTAINS BICARBONATE OF SODA, PHOSPHATE, & SALT
MANUFACTURED BY
CHELSEA MILLING CO.
CHELSEA MICH.

seriously damaged the mill. News of the fire ran in the December 10 issue of the *Chelsea Standard-Herald:*

> *The fire at the mill last Saturday so frightened Mr. Hatch, the proprietor, that he had to be taken home, where he still remains quite ill.*

Mr. Hatch never did recover—financially, anyway—from the fire. Following the disaster, an entrepreneurial miller named Enos K. White bought what was left of the Chelsea Steam Roller Mill.

According to White's grandson, Dudley (Kirke) Holmes Sr., "Enos

THE CHELSEA FIRE DEPARTMENT IN 1909, PAUSING AFTER TRAINING EXERCISES. LONGTIME FIRE CHIEF HOWARD BROOKS, IN A WHITE STRAW HAT, STANDS FRONT AND CENTER. YEARS LATER, CHELSEA MILLING EMPLOYEES WOULD SERVE AS VOLUNTEER FIREFIGHTERS.

Kirke White owned several mills in Illinois, Indiana, and Michigan. He bought and sold them and loved to move around, apparently. At one time he owned five or six milling companies. Chelsea was just one stop in his career. My Grandfather White was a very well-informed man, enjoyed people, and made friends easily."

When E. K. White arrived in Chelsea to run the mill, he brought two pretty daughters with him. One of them was named Mabel.

A New Century Begins
Chelsea's Mill Unites the White and Holmes Families

Enos K. White, his wife, and two daughters settled in a house on the corner of East Middle Street, three doors away from an elaborate Victorian home that had been built by a successful Chelsea businessman by the name of Harmon S. Holmes.

White's newly acquired mill was one of more than 700 flour, feed, and gristmills in Michigan; 130 of them were roller mills with a daily capacity of 20,000 barrels. He bought the mill near the time when the Millers' National Association announced that flour milling had become the nation's largest single industry. Michigan ranked tenth in the nation in flour mills, boasting an annual production of four million barrels of flour. The average price paid for a bushel of wheat was 69 cents; the average price for a barrel of flour, $3.73. Clearly, milling was a big business in a prosperous period. The old-time gristmill had, over a relatively short period of time, grown from a cottage industry into big business.

Recognizing a growing industry when he saw one, Harmon Holmes began investing in the White Milling Company in 1898.

"My Grandfather Holmes was quite a versatile person business-wise," Dudley Holmes Sr. once said. "He invested in many local businesses. He would be a silent partner."

(ABOVE) HARMON S. HOLMES SERVED AS A SILENT PARTNER IN THE WHITE MILLING COMPANY IN THE EARLY 1900S. AFTER WHITE'S MILL SUFFERED A DEVASTATING FIRE, HOLMES PURCHASED THE BUSINESS OUTRIGHT.

"He was an extraordinary bookkeeper—and a very astute investor," observed Sandy Schultz, longtime Chelsea Milling Company employee. (Schultz was executive assistant to both the second and third men named Howard Holmes.) She has studied Harmon's investments as recorded in the company archives. "He had a separate envelope listing every loan or investment he ever made—and there were many of them. On the outside, in tiny, meticulous handwriting, Harmon would write the dates of the transactions. As soon as he invested, he took out an insurance policy to guarantee his money, should the owner default. We have boxes and boxes of these envelopes."

The Chelsea Milling Company also has copies of Harmon Holmes's stock certificates for the White Milling Company; shares were ten dollars

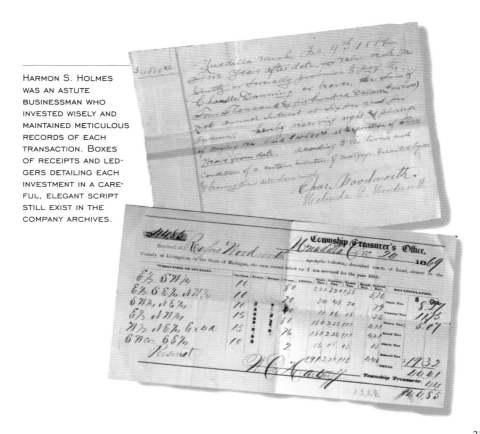

HARMON S. HOLMES WAS AN ASTUTE BUSINESSMAN WHO INVESTED WISELY AND MAINTAINED METICULOUS RECORDS OF EACH TRANSACTION. BOXES OF RECEIPTS AND LEDGERS DETAILING EACH INVESTMENT IN A CAREFUL, ELEGANT SCRIPT STILL EXIST IN THE COMPANY ARCHIVES.

Chelsea Standard-Herald
July 26, 1906

Mr. E. K. White Has Had The Chelsea Flouring Mills Thoroughly Overhauled Recently.

During the past three months, E. K. White, owner of the Chelsea Flouring Mills, has had the mill thoroughly overhauled and expended a large sum of money for new equipment.

One of the most notable changes has taken place on the top floor of the building where the flour is bolted. Under the present arrangement two bolting or sifting machines have been installed that will do the work of thirty-two of the old style sifters that were used in the plant before. Another new device added is a steam heating apparatus that is used for toughening the bran of the wheat, and an automatic machine that regulates the feeding of the grain to rolls is another of the additions. Mr. White has also installed what is known by millers as a wheat grader, that will separate all of the poor quality of grain from the good.

The old tin spouts that have been in the mill for years have been replaced with new ones made of wood. Every piece of machinery that is in the plant is of the latest construction and the work has been done under the charge of thorough millwrights.

Mr. White informs the Standard Herald *that he has been milling for the past thirty-seven years, and that in all of his experience he has never seen anything in the shape of flour that will begin to compare with the present output of the Chelsea Flour Mill with its new milling machinery.*

apiece, and Harmon would buy anywhere from two to ten shares at a time. His financial investment apparently gave White the opportunity to upgrade and modernize the mill with the latest improvements in equipment, which resulted in a very high grade of flour.

With the new equipment installed, the mill was poised for big business and ran the following advertisement:

> *THE CHELSEA FLOUR MILLS are now ready for business after a shutdown of three months to install new machinery. We now have the finest flour machinery made and will be glad to have farmers bring us their wheat to exchange for flour. We are putting in a wheat grader. We can handle your wheat—no matter how badly shrunken, and pay you the market price, as we clean it for you and return you the screenings. We now have more bran and middlings than this community can use and will sell it to you right. Give us a call before selling your grain. Ask your grocery for White's Best Patent and Tip Top Flour.*
> —*E. K. White*

E. K. White must have been excited and optimistic about the future of White Milling Company when he placed this ad, but his optimism didn't last long. Within six months, the mill suffered from what must have been another devastating fire, although few details remain. The January 3, 1907, issue of the newspaper reported that White had placed an order for new roller feed-grinding machinery.

"Meanwhile," according to the paper, "Mr. White will for the present place a temporary covering over the engine room of the old mill that was burned and do feed grinding." Nothing more is known about this fire, but soon afterward E. K. White agreed to sell the business outright to Harmon Holmes, and the White family left Chelsea to move on to another mill in Findlay, Ohio.

Harmon incorporated the mill under the name of the Wm. Bacon-Holmes Company and became the first of four generations of the Holmes family to own the Chelsea mill. His partner, William

WM. BACON - HOLMES COMPANY,
WHOLESALERS AND RETAILERS OF ALL KINDS OF
Lumber, Building Material, Coal, Coke, Charcoal, Lime, Cement, Roofing, Wool, Salt,
Seed and Grain, Graham, Corn Meal, Middlings and Bran.

FROM
Wm. Bacon-Holmes Co.
Chelsea, Michigan
TO

Bacon, was another Chelsea entrepreneur with many interests in local businesses. He and Harmon were already partners in a business that produced lumber, coal, lime, cement, salt, and wood, and raised poultry. And both were also involved in Chelsea's Kempf Bank.

Harmon launched a major building project shortly after purchasing the mill, probably to replace the equipment and structure destroyed by the fire. He hired the Meisel Company of Port Huron to construct a mill capable of producing forty barrels of flour a day. "In equipment, the mill will have nothing but the best—the same as is used in the greatest flouring mills of the country," he told the *Chelsea Standard-Herald*.

Harmon's new mill processed both red and white wheat into pastry "patented" flour sold under the Phoenix label. All-purpose flour, a blend of hard wheat and soft wheat, was sold under the name of Acme. This flour became a favorite of local housewives, who believed that it made "excessively good" bread and biscuits.

WILLIAM BACON WAS A CHELSEA ENTREPRENEUR WITH INTERESTS IN MANY CHELSEA BUSINESSES.

THE FIRST HOLMES AT THE HELM

The Harmon S. Holmes story

One of ten children, Harmon Holmes was born in 1854 to Samuel Wygant and Francis Cornelia (Peters) Holmes of Macon, Michigan. His father held an interest in one of the first gristmills in Washtenaw County, Michigan, under the partnership of Peters & Holmes. Samuel undoubtedly set the example for his enterprising son by eventually adding mills under the same partnership in Dexter, Dover, and Scio.

Harmon left home at the age of eighteen and quickly embarked on his own business career. He moved to Chelsea where he formed and dissolved various partnerships in enterprises from clothing, farm implements, hardware, dry goods, furniture, lumber, coal, beans, and grains.

His first partnership, with Thomas Wilkinson, resulted in the formation of the general store Wilkinson & Holmes. That association was maintained for two years until March 21, 1874, when Harmon sold out. In August 1874, he engaged in business as a member of the firm of Durand, Holmes & Company, carrying a general line of goods and continuing until 1880, when the senior partner sold his interest to

MACON, MICHIGAN, NATIVE HARMON S. HOLMES (ABOVE) ARRIVED IN CHELSEA WHEN HE WAS EIGHTEEN. THERE HE MARRIED TWICE, RAISED HIS CHILDREN, PARTICIPATED IN LOCAL POLITICS AND COMMUNITY EVENTS, HEADED A BANK AND NUMEROUS BUSINESS VENTURES, AND INVESTED IN MANY LOCAL BUSINESSES.

THE H. S. HOLMES MERCANTILE & GENERAL STORE (FIRST LOWERED AWNING) WAS LOCATED ON MAIN STREET JUST SOUTH OF MIDDLE STREET IN THE EARLY 1900s.

B. Parker and the firm of Holmes & Parker was formed. That relationship lasted until spring 1888, after which Harmon was alone in the conduct of the business until 1904, when the H. S. Holmes Mercantile Company was organized, providing employment to about twelve people. It became one of the largest and most profitable commercial interests in Chelsea.

Not content to rest on past achievements, Harmon added to his business holdings by joining with E. G. Hoag in 1890 to form the firm of Hoag & Holmes, dealers in hardware, farm implements, and furniture. In this enterprise Harmon continued until 1902, when the business became the property of Holmes & Walker. During this period, Harmon became actively connected with the Kempf Commercial & Savings Bank, obtaining the position of president by 1899. He also became a stockholder and director in the Chelsea Savings Bank.

On April 25, 1901, the *Chelsea Standard-Herald* reported that the firm of Kempf & Company was dissolved and the Wm. Bacon-Holmes Company had been incorporated to take its place. Harmon was president, J. A. Palmer and R. D. Walker served as vice presidents, William Bacon

JUST because a coat is a *raincoat* is no reason why it can't be a truly stylish light overcoat—as the Kuppenheimer Watershed *proves*.

Let us show you one—and demonstrate the difference.

SOLD EXCLUSIVELY BY

H. S. Holmes Mercantile Co.

CHELSEA, MICH.

was secretary and manager, and George A. Begole was named treasurer.

After forming the Wm. Bacon-Holmes Company, which included the Chelsea mill, Harmon invested in the firm of Dancer Brogan & Company of Lansing, dealers in dry goods. But his chief attention was reserved for the banking business, and under his guidance a safe and conservative policy was followed.

Harmon Holmes was well thought of and respected in both the business and social communities. In addition to his obvious success, he maintained an integrity and sense of honor that set the tone for future generations of the Holmes family.

The 1905 publication *Past and Present of Washtenaw County* provides an intriguing picture of Harmon's professional as well as personal reputation:

> *H. S. Holmes . . . possesses that keen insight into business conditions and ready adaptability which are the foundation of all success. Moreover his business methods have been so honorable and his activity so continuous that he has gained an untarnished name and at the same time a gratifying measure of prosperity. . . .*
>
> *Mr. Holmes is a man of resourceful business ability and broad capacity for the successful establishment and conduct of commercial interests. . . . In his political views, Mr. Holmes has always been a Republican. He has served as a member of the board of trustees and as president of the school board and was appointed on the board of control*

of Michigan state prison. . . . Fraternally he is a Mason. . . . He is likewise connected with the Knights of Pythias. . . . His entire career is illustrative of the fact that certain actions are followed by certain results. In business he has been a promoter of successful enterprises that have contributed to general prosperity as well as to individual success and as a citizen he is an illustration of a high type of our American manhood.

"I have always been intrigued by the patriarch of the Holmes family, Harmon S. Holmes," said Chelsea attorney John Keusch, who was born in town in 1910 and remembered Mr. Holmes well. "As a kid, I remember seeing him sitting at his desk in the Kempf Bank. He also ran a store with Mr. Vogel, a big operation. A lot of people got their start in business thanks to Mr. Holmes. I remember him as a small, meticulously dressed man who always carried a cane.

"Mr. Holmes evidently saw more economic opportunity here in Chelsea, and he came here at an early age, bringing all kinds of relatives with him," recalled Keusch. "Mr. Wurster, who ran the clothing store, was his nephew. Charlie Martin, who ran the livery stable, was his brother-in-law. Dennis Walker, who established Walker Hardware Store, was another brother-in-law," continued Keusch. "Harmon Holmes was also related to Senator Royal Copeland of New York, who had been mayor of Ann Arbor at one time."

Harmon had married at an early age, and his first wife and child died during childbirth. His second wife, Edith, bore him four children (a son died in infancy) and they lived in the Victorian home Harmon built on Middle Street in Chelsea. It was while living there that Harmon's son Howard became acquainted with Miss Mabel White, who lived on the same block.

The Holmes family was well-known in town, and notices in the local newspaper often gave small but intriguing glimpses into the prominent family's private life:

H. S. Holmes will leave next Saturday eve for New York and Boston, where he will be about ten days purchasing dry goods for his extensive trade. Look out for new goods about September 5.
—August 1, 1880

We omitted to mention in our last issue that H. S. Holmes, our dry goods merchant, has been quite ill for nearly two weeks, with rheumatism and a slight indication of fever, but is now convalescent.
—February 17, 1881

The newspaper also reported on Harmon and Edith's tenth anniversary celebration in their home on October 15, 1889:

One of the most joyful events, the celebrating of a wedding anniversary, occurred in this village last Tuesday evening, at the

THE GRAY VICTORIAN MANSION BUILT BY HARMON S. HOLMES ON EAST MIDDLE STREET QUICKLY
BECAME A CHELSEA VILLAGE LANDMARK. IT SERVED AS THE HOME OF FOUR GENERATIONS OF THE
HOLMES FAMILY. IN ITS KITCHEN, MABEL WHITE HOLMES DEVELOPED JIFFY BISCUIT MIX,
LAUNCHING AMERICA'S PACKAGED-MIX INDUSTRY.

*pleasant and beautiful home of Mr. and Mrs. H. S. Holmes, on Middle
Street, East.*

    *Monday evening, two ladies passed around in the community
inviting acquaintances to meet at the Chelsea House, Tuesday evening,
from which place a procession was formed, all marching to the residence
of Mr. Holmes. Upon ringing the doorbell, Mrs. Holmes appeared and
a more surprised person would be hard to find. However, she gave
each one a hearty welcome, and made all to feel at home and at ease.
Mr. Holmes being up town, a self appointed committee went in search
of him and triumphantly brought him down. The evening passed
very pleasantly, Miss Lucy E. Lowe furnishing instrumental music.
. . . Just before adjourning to the dining room, Rev. Thos. Holmes, in
such appropriate words as only he can find, presented Mr. and Mrs.
Holmes with a most handsome silver tea set of seven pieces, as a slight
token of esteem by those present, and as a memento of this, the tenth*

anniversary of their married life.

The dining room table was loaded down with such viands as only our Chelsea ladies know how to prepare, and as with the little boy we thought, "we get full before we have half enough."

After lunch, those so inclined wended their way to the smoking room up the stairs, and puffed the pure Havana, while the ladies talked and visited below, and "us" younger ones took in the second table.

To linger long after lunch would have been a breach of good breeding, as the clock indicated nearly 12. So bidding the honored host and hostess good-night, and wishing them many returns of the day, all departed for their respective homes, feeling that the evening had been spent in a most enjoyable manner.

An August 8, 1901, story headlined "Holmes Gets Deed on Record First" reveals that sometimes brothers-in-law are not the best of friends:

This week saw a hot race between John J. Tuomey of Detroit, and Harmon S. Holmes of Chelsea to get their respective deeds on record covering the same piece of property.

Mr. Tuomey married Mr. Holmes' sister and the race between the brothers-in-law was very exciting while it lasted.

The property in question is the land known as the Samuel H. Holmes farm in Scio and consists of 127 acres. According to the deeds in question, Mrs. Tuomey deeded her right and title in this property to her husband and also to her brother.

On the night of July 30, Mr. Tuomey came at a late hour and requested Deputy Seerey to file his deed. Mr. Seerey saw that the document was not properly acknowledged and was lacking one witness. He pointed out the defect to Mr. Tuomey and the latter took it away with him to have it remedied.

Bright and early the next morning Mr. Holmes' deed appeared in the office and it was properly recorded. The morning following Mr. Tuomey showed up with his deed and it was recorded, but as Mr. Holmes' document was recorded first the title must vest in him unless the courts decree otherwise.

Undoubtedly litigation will result as Mr. Tuomey seemed to be much perturbed over the turn of affairs.

"My great-grandfather, Harmon S. Holmes, was the classic Victorian banker, complete with formal attire and a cane," recalled the third Howard Holmes (Howdy). "He was involved in many businesses, but banking was his real love. He was a silent partner in the mill—his involvement was strictly financial."

"I remember Mr. Harmon S. Holmes," said Claude Sears Rogers, the boyhood friend of Harmon's twin grandsons, Howard and Dudley. "He was a very sedate, calm man. He had an impressive mustache. I remember his visage. He was very well respected and a very successful businessman. He had an office in the bank, and the twins would just walk past the tellers and customers up to his desk. He'd give them a dime and they'd leave happy. I went with them once. I was quite impressed!"

Harmon's primary focus had always been banking. And there may have been a reason for his preference for three-piece suits and gold-tipped walking canes. The fact is that Harmon had gained some hands-on experience of hard labor from his mother's brothers, George Augustus and Henry Peters. Their father, George W. Peters, had built and operated the Hudson Milling Company, one of the very first gristmills in Washtenaw County. George W. Peter's daughter, Francis Cornelia Peters, married Samuel Wygant Holmes, and their son Harmon became a frequent visitor (and possibly an occasional laborer) at the Scio Flour Mill back in the days when mills were not much more than grinding stones and sweat. Although Harmon saw potential in the milling business, he must have had his fill of working in one as a boy. As soon as his son Howard was ready, Harmon turned over the day-to-day operation of the Chelsea mill to him.

HARMON S. HOLMES'S FATHER, SAMUEL WYGANT HOLMES, INVESTED IN THE HUDSON MILLING COMPANY, FORMING THE PARTNERSHIP OF PETERS & HOLMES. HE EVENTUALLY MARRIED INTO THE PETERS FAMILY.

$590 1911 **FORD Model T Torpedo**

4 Cylinders, 2 Passengers Two 6-inch Gas Lamps. Generator
Completely equipped as follows: Three Oil Lamps
Extension Top. Speedometer Horn and Tools
Automatic Brass Windshield Ford Magneto built into the motor
This car thus fully equipped for $590, F. O. B. Detroit

THE DEAL THAT GOT AWAY!

Dudley Holmes Sr. remembered his grandfather Harmon Holmes as "a very intellectual person, the kind of man that everyone came to when they had a problem of any sort because they trusted his advice and his opinions. He was extremely well-informed and had seemingly countless involvements in the community and the business world. He was a substantial, imposing figure. He was a leader."

But the best story passed down about Harmon Holmes doesn't focus on his intellect or his many financial successes. Instead, it reveals a family secret about a very big business deal that got away. "Somehow, Henry Ford knew Harmon—how, I don't know," explained his great-grandson Howdy. "My father loved to tell the story of the day in the early 1900s when Henry Ford visited Harmon at the bank. Apparently, Henry asked Harmon to be one of the original investors in the Ford Motor Company for a twenty-five percent interest. In that age before automobiles, Harmon Holmes responded in a paraphrased, 'Are you kidding?' Apparently, Harmon didn't think the automobile was a great idea—which perplexes me, because he seemed to be a true entrepreneur, with his fingers in many businesses. I've often wondered exactly what was said and why. It's one of the stories that families cherish—and groan about," recalled Howdy with amusement.

THE SECOND GENERATION

Howard Samuel Holmes Takes the Reins

HOWARD SAMUEL HOLMES.

One of four children born to Harmon and Edith Holmes, Howard Samuel Holmes was the only one to stay in Chelsea as an adult and actively participate in his father's many business enterprises. A quiet man, always immaculately and formally dressed, Howard was known throughout Michigan as a kind man with a heart for the milling business.

Howard managed to accomplish something a long succession of nineteenth-century mill owners had tried, but failed, to do. He established a strong and successful business that was able to weather wars, recessions, depressions, fires, accidents, and family tragedies. And his efforts ensured that the company would remain within the family from that generation on.

"My father, Howard, was quite different from his father, although he too enjoyed a good standing among the business community," Dudley Holmes Sr. observed. "Harmon had quite a commanding presence and could be intimidating. Unlike his father, Howard focused his attention and professional energies on the mill, rather than the other enterprises my grandfather had established."

After graduating from the University of Michigan with a degree in literature in 1907, Howard accepted a job as an assistant cashier in the

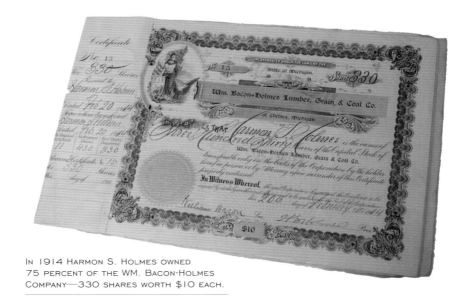

IN 1914 HARMON S. HOLMES OWNED
75 PERCENT OF THE WM. BACON-HOLMES
COMPANY—330 SHARES WORTH $10 EACH.

Kempf Bank, which his father headed. But he didn't stay there long. One biography explains that Howard found bank work "too confining for his temperament." After resigning, he moved on to the Wm. Bacon-Holmes Company ("Purveyors of Lumber, Coal, Lime, Cement, Salt, Wood, Poultry and all kinds of Seed & Grain"). For a time, Howard served as secretary, treasurer, and general manager of the odd conglomerate.

"My grandfather [Harmon] was certainly very capable of managing the mill along with everything else, but he believed in training people and letting them handle what they did best," said Dudley Holmes Sr. "He turned the mill over to my father, who seemed to have more of a heart for it than my grandfather did."

Several years after Howard took over management of the mill, he prepared for a merger of a more personal nature. The *Chelsea Standard* of February 8, 1912, announced that Howard entertained thirty-five friends at a supper celebrating his approaching marriage to Miss Mabel White. Even though the Whites had moved to Ohio after selling the mill, Howard had apparently kept in touch with his childhood sweetheart.

Three days after the dinner, a small newspaper article carried the following announcement:

White-Holmes Wedding

The marriage of Miss Mabel White and Mr. Howard Holmes of this place will take place at the home of the bride's parents, Mr. and Mrs. E. K. White of Findlay, Ohio, at 7:30 o'clock this Thursday evening. The ceremony will be attended by Miss Estella White, sister of the bride, and Mr. Chas. B. Franklin, of Denver, Colorado. Mr. and Mrs. H. S. Holmes, parents of the groom, Mrs. D. C. McLaren and Miss Beryl McNamara of this place will be present.

After a short wedding trip the couple will be at home to their friends on McKinley Street in the residence which the groom has just built.

The marriage united the two Midwestern milling families and set the stage for Mabel's significant contribution to the milling industry. A year later, in the summer of 1913, Mabel gave birth to twin sons, Dudley and Howard.

MR. AND MRS. E. K. WHITE WITH THEIR TWIN GRANDSONS, HOWARD AND DUDLEY.

Improvements and additions to the mill continued under Howard's guidance. In its annual statement on January 1, 1917, the company announced that an addition costing $1,110.42 had been completed and estimated that the mill was worth $7,426.48. Shortly afterward, the business was reorganized. The mill was separated from the other components, and Howard was made president of the newly named Chelsea Roller Mills, a division of the Wm. Bacon-Holmes Company.

When World War I broke out in Europe, the Chelsea Roller Mills ran night and day to supply wheat for the American army and its European allies. In order to feed the soldiers, the United States government imposed a long list of new rules, regulations, and restrictions on mills. "Our industry fared quite well and was able to operate at pretty full capacity," historian Fred N. Rowe later wrote.

The war continued to influence the milling industry long after the last guns were fired and the last veteran returned home. The wartime regulations had laid the foundation for future federal controls. Throughout the 1920s, the Millers' National Federation (formerly the Millers' National Association) analyzed changes in both the milling business and the American way of life. Their greatest concerns were the "elimination of capacity, the development of concentrated buying, the decline in home baking, the decline in per capita consumption of flour, and speculation in wheat."

Harmon Samuel Holmes died of pernicious anemia in a Battle Creek sanatorium on Monday morning, January 2, 1922, seven years after his second wife, Edith, had passed away. Harmon was survived by his sons Howard S. and Ralph (who worked for a food company in Battle Creek), his daughter, Mrs. Enid Ellis of Grand Rapids, and his two grandsons, Howard and Dudley Holmes. The *Chelsea Standard* reported:

> *The funeral was held from the late residence at 3 o'clock Wednesday afternoon, Rev. P. W. Dierberger of South Haven, assisted by Rev. E. A. Cannes, pastor of the Chelsea Congregational Church, conducting the services. Burial at Oak Grove Cemetery. The members of the Masonic Order attended the services in a body and conducted the burial service of the order at the grave.*

Employees of the Wm. Bacon-Holmes Company were given the day off, so they could pay their respects to Harmon S. Holmes.

In 1923, shortly after Harmon's death, the company's name was changed to the Chelsea Milling Company. Howard at that time was officially the secretary of the new mill and he set out to remodel and remold the business. He started by establishing a very advantageous

Harmon S. Holmes with his grandsons Howard (left) and Dudley.

friendship with C. F. Smith, who owned a line of supermarkets and bakeries in Detroit. C. F. Smith became the company's earliest and strongest customer.

"Old Mr. Holmes died before he could realize the vision of his 'spendthrift' son," said former employee Roy Ives. "Howard completely remodeled the mill in the early 1920s by installing the most modern wheat grain cleaning and tempering equipment available. Howard installed twelve multiple grinding stands, each with two pairs of rollers, plus the sifters, middling purifiers, flour purifiers, and grading reels necessary for patented flour grading." The milling capacity grew from 45 to 350 barrels a day, recalled Ives.

After his father's death, Howard balanced his energies between running business at the mill and enjoying time with his family. "Mr. Howard Holmes was a very conscientious businessperson and a wonderful man, the finest gentleman," remembered Claude Sears Rogers. "I would say that he was a model gentleman. He was wonderful with his employees and he was wonderful with 'The Boys' "—that's how everyone in town referred to Howard and Dudley, even long after their boyhood.

Howard's energetic twin boys were a challenge to raise as well as a constant source of entertainment. As in any childhood, mischief was ever present, but with twins it was often double trouble. Many acquaintances of The Boys have been eager to share stories that have endured through the years.

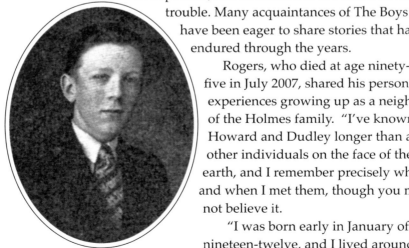

CLAUDE SEARS ROGERS.

Rogers, who died at age ninety-five in July 2007, shared his personal experiences growing up as a neighbor of the Holmes family. "I've known Howard and Dudley longer than any other individuals on the face of the earth, and I remember precisely where and when I met them, though you may not believe it.

"I was born early in January of nineteen-twelve, and I lived around the corner from the Holmes's house

on East Middle Street. One sunny summer day when I was just about two-and-a-half years old, my mother took me for a walk. As we came around the corner of East Middle Street, I saw a nursemaid with twin babies, and I was very impressed with a carriage for two."

In time their friendship flourished, and Rogers and his brother, Dean, regularly called on "Howd" and "Dud" when they were ripe for adventure. Once they all tried digging to China from under the Holmes's front porch. Another time they stole a cigar from Grandfather Holmes and tried smoking—"That didn't last any longer than the moment when Dean turned green," recalled Rogers.

Dudley's daughter Diane Hall shared several stories about her father and uncle. Once when company was expected for dinner, The Boys, already dressed in their Sunday best, found the day's egg delivery on the porch and decided to have an egg fight in the vestibule. Broken eggs covered everything, from the ceiling to the twins.

Another time, when The Boys were about eight years old and Harmon Holmes was living with them, he caught them swimming in the basement cistern. Harmon had kept his cigars near the cistern because of the natural humidity, and when he went down to get one he found

THE HOLMES FAMILY SPENT SUMMERS AT NEARBY CAVANAUGH LAKE DURING THE 1920S AND 1930S. IT WAS A COMMON SIGHT TO SEE DUDLEY (RIGHT) AND HOWARD ON THEIR PONIES AS THEY RACED THE FOUR MILES FROM THE FAMILY FARM ON NORTH MAIN STREET TO THE LAKE COTTAGE.

the twins swimming in the family's drinking water! Grandfather Holmes was quick to correct them, and it was never spoken of again.

The Boys would often try to fool people, including their parents, about which twin was which. Mabel made a special pie for each twin. Howard's favorite was apple and Dudley's was pumpkin. One evening the boys sat down on purpose at the wrong seat in front of the wrong pie, hoping to fool their parents. Of course, Mabel and Howard knew what was going on and later had a private laugh.

Often it took awhile for even close friends to know for sure which twin they were talking to. "It was in small ways that they differed," explained Claude Rogers. "Dudley's jaw was a little squarer than Howard's. Their mannerisms were different. Howard was a better student than Dudley, a little more conservative than Dudley. That didn't mean that Dud wasn't as smart. He just didn't like to study the way Howard did. Dudley was definitely more risky and risqué about things. He'd rather have fun than study."

Occasionally they used their identical looks for some "deviltry," Rogers recalled. "To show you how much alike they were, I'll tell you a story. Dud and I would go to Jackson once in awhile at night, and Dud got to know a girl up there. One time—I don't know why—Dudley

HOLDAYS WERE SPECIAL OCCASIONS, AND HOLMES FAMILY MEMBERS OFTEN CELEBRATED AT THE FARM OR AT CAVANAUGH LAKE. HERE THE TWINS RIDE A TEAM OF OXEN WHILE THEIR FATHER, HOWARD HOLMES, WAVES THE FLAG DURING A PATRIOTIC HOLIDAY.

couldn't go, and Howard wanted to go in his place. I clued Howard in to her name. That night Howard and I followed the same routine Dudley and I did. We drove the girls around town and had a beer. That girl spent the whole evening with Howard and didn't know the difference."

The Boys were also regular visitors to their father's mill throughout their youth. The mill was a place of endless fascination for any young boy. "I literally grew up at the mill," wrote Roy Ives, who was born in 1911. "I was a small lad, between nine and twelve, when I was in Chelsea. My father, Wirt Ives, worked first as the gristmill operator and later operated the wheat receiving and cleaning portion of Mr. Holmes's mill. I was intrigued with the mill's operation and spent many fascinating hours roaming the mill." Ives often explored the mill with Howard and Dudley, who were a few years younger than Ives. As a result, the twins were well-indoctrinated into all the workings and every secret corner of the mill.

Sports were other favorite pastimes for The Boys. They enjoyed golf, swimming, and horseback riding. During the 1920s and 1930s, it was a common sight on a summer night to see Dudley and Howard on their

ponies as they raced the four miles from the family farm to their cottage at Cavanaugh Lake. Many times they played basketball in the upper story of the barn or golf on the three-hole course their father built on his farm. Throughout their school years both were talented football and basketball players.

Athletic activities were different from how they are today, and players often found themselves in amusing circumstances. Diane Hall remembers two football-related stories from the twins' high school years. Back then, Chelsea High School games were played on the Holmes farm in the same field where cattle grazed everyday. Before the game could be played, the players had to remove the "cow pies." The tradition was that the best scholars on the team would be sent to the field prior to the game and given the honor of getting it ready. Howard's excellent scholastic record usually landed him on the list for manure removal. Dudley, on the other hand, happily avoided the honor.

During the Depression there wasn't a lot of money for sports, and equipment was scarce. The team had only one football to use in practice and one football for the game, and both had to last for the entire season. Dudley Sr. recalled for his daughter Diane that there had been only one regulation helmet for the entire team. Once a play had been decided on, the ball carrier almost always wore the good helmet. This presented an opportunity for some interesting fake plays, but also assured that the wearer of the helmet

was pummeled, whether or not he was carrying the ball.

Howard's athletic record was impressive. He was captain of the football team both junior and senior year and played basketball all four years in high school, taking the district title in 1931. In addition to his athletic prowess, he was an accomplished orator, actor, journalist, and class leader. He was editor-in-chief of the yearbook his senior year, class president his sophomore and junior years, and an award-winning orator of his graduating class. The inscription on Howard's senior picture reads: "Here's to a man who will make us proud; his name they'll shout both long and loud."

Dudley matched Howard's athletic record by playing basketball all four years and serving as team captain his senior year; he also played football for three years. And like his twin, Dudley enjoyed acting in school plays. In his senior year he took up business-management studies. Dudley's high school years in many ways were a blueprint for his subsequent life. Dudley's quick wit and biting humor made him very popular with his classmates. In his senior yearbook, Dudley willed to an underclassman his "wit and sarcasm not yet expended." Next to his senior picture are the words: "An answer for every passing remark, popular, witty, and a regular 'spark.'"

"The Boys were well-raised and well cared for," observed Claude Rogers. "They had a sound upbringing by their parents. They had high moral standards. They had honor, intelligence, and education. They would never think of doing an underhanded thing. They were taught to be careful about money, not to squander it," Rogers said. "They were

IN 1929 THE CHELSEA BULLDOGS HAD FRESHMEN TAKE TO THE BASKETBALL COURT. THE TEAM INCLUDED HOWARD (FRONT ROW, SECOND FROM LEFT) AND DUDLEY (FRONT ROW, SECOND FROM RIGHT). THAT YEAR CHELSEA SCORED 441 POINTS TO THE OPPONENTS' 303 POINTS, WINNING 13 OUT OF 17 GAMES.

well-taught about wealth and not showing off. Throughout their lives, they retained what they were taught. They were raised differently from the other boys in town. Their father was an excellent role model."

In early 1929, things were going smoothly for the Holmes family. The first Howard was comfortably entering middle age and his twin sons were popular with their classmates and friends and excelling on many levels in high school. Then, without warning, on October 29, the stock market crashed.

Unlike many of their neighbors and friends, the Holmes family remained relatively untouched by the ensuing Depression. "People have to eat," Dudley Sr. pointed out seventy years later, explaining why the family business survived. "You can do without many things if you have to, but food is not one of them."

But Howard's goal was not just to see his family comfortably through the Depression. He was determined to keep everyone at

DUDLEY (FAR RIGHT) PLAYED LEFT END AND HOWARD (BOTTOM ROW, CENTER) PLAYED QUARTERBACK ON THE 1929 BULLDOGS' FOOTBALL TEAM.

Chelsea Milling employed. Throughout the dark days that followed, Howard continued to operate Chelsea Milling at full power. He sold his flour to individual consumers in 100-, 50-, 20-, 10-, 5-, and 2 ½-pound bags. Flour for bakers was packed in 100- and 140-pound bags. When times were slow at the mill, Howard would ask the women employees to clean the plant, and he would send the men to work in the onion fields on the Holmes farm just north of town.

"The wages at Chelsea Milling Company were low compared to the auto industry, but there were no layoffs during slack periods or reduced work weeks," Roy Ives remembered. "That was very important to the people who worked here." For this reason many local residents turned to the mill for employment. Throughout the 1930s, the line of job applicants would sometimes start at the door and stretch along the front of the plant.

Veryl Hafley was one of the few people fortunate enough to get a job at the mill in those years. "You had to know someone to get in here," he recalled. "My oldest brother worked here. It was a good job because it was steady. I came to the mill when I was a kid, working nights after school. I stayed until the war broke out, then came back afterwards. We were all proud of the fact that the mill never laid one person off all through the Depression."

Bob Howe worked in the flour mill during the Depression years. "I had a different job every day," he remembered. "The head miller was usually the boss, and he told us all what to do. One day I'd pack feed, the next I might load flour, work in the warehouse, or take the wheat from the boxcars. Those were the days when we were just milling flour and Howard Holmes ran Chelsea Milling. He was an excellent man to work for—a very fair man."

Howard Holmes was as conservative in business as he was generous in private, his employees knew. "Mr. Holmes did not attempt to buy 'futures.' He did not gamble with the ups and downs of the stock market," Roy Ives explained. "He always hedged any purchase by selling the same amount. He knew the cost of his raw materials and could plan to have wheat on hand for all projected sales."

Howard capitalized on the mill's strategic location along the Michigan Central Railroad tracks, said Ives. "There was a peculiarity of the tariff regulations called 'Milling in Transit.' As long as the wheat grain and its finished product, flour, continued in the same direction in which it entered the municipality, the tariff rate was less. Hard spring wheat from Kansas (Turkey Red variety) or Minnesota could be routed on the south branch of the New York Central from Chicago and arrive in Chelsea from the west, giving an advantageous freight rate. I know this for a fact because I was doing this bookkeeping in 1930 and 1931."

Howard's business savvy definitely contributed to the survival of the mill. Thousands of mills—large and small—shut down during the Depression. The profit margin in milling flour was very small industry-wide, but Howard "seemed to have a magic touch in purchasing raw materials, shipping, milling, and distributing to advantage," recalled Ives. As a result Chelsea's mill not only survived, but also managed to provide its employees with steady work throughout the 1930s.

Unfortunately for farmers the Depression didn't end until World War II. "Times were hard right up until 1941," remembered Donna Lane. In 1900 a bushel of wheat had sold for 69 cents; in 1931 the price

HOWARD SAMUEL HOLMES WITH HIS SISTER-IN-LAW, ESTELLE B. WHITE, AND HIS SONS, HOWARD (LEFT) AND DUDLEY.

plummeted to 35 cents. Lane's father raised sixty-five or seventy acres of wheat on a tenant farm near North Lake. "That was his cash crop," she said. "The wheat harvest took place sometime around July nineteenth. Farmers planted winter wheat in the fall, so that way they could get two crops every year, you see. As a little girl I'd watch my dad get ready to load his old Chevy truck with his wheat, then head off to the Chelsea mill. He'd bring sixty- or one-hundred-pound bags of wheat, and in exchange, they'd give him flour." Lane also remembered stopping at a bakery in the little country town of Leslie when her mother sold wool to a mill in Eaton Rapids, because that bakery used Chelsea flour.

Despite the loyalty demonstrated by community members like Donna Lane's family, Howard struggled to keep the mill going through the difficult times, which saw bank foreclosures, personal and corporate bankruptcies, widespread unemployment, and a drought that devastated

Chelsea High School, Chelsea, Michigan,

the crops of local farmers, already hurting from seriously reduced prices.

Employees who worked at Chelsea Milling during that dark time always remained proud of the way the mill had been run. Years later when members of the next generation came to work at the mill, they did so in part because they remembered the community pride their parents had felt in working together to survive a difficult period.

The second Howard Holmes observed years later, "I think the

THE CHELSEA HIGH SCHOOL SENIOR CLASS OF 1931 TRAVELED TO WASHINGTON D.C. IN
JUNE FOR THEIR CLASS TRIP AND POSED IN FRONT OF THE CAPITOL BUILDING. HOWARD (LEFT)
AND DUDLEY (RIGHT) FLANKED THE CLASS IN THE FRONT ROW.

positive attitude of the workers and the atmosphere [at the mill], which
have prevailed through the years, can be taken back to both my mother
and my father [Mabel and the first Howard Holmes]. They always felt
that everybody was equal, regardless of his job, and they did their best
to treat everyone evenhandedly."

JIFFY RAISES PROFITS
The Mill Expands to Meet Growing Demand

Business took a new and welcome turn for the better when Mabel White Holmes developed the nation's first packaged mix. The JIFFY Biscuit Mix predated its competitors by at least six months. C. F. Smith Company of Detroit was the first customer to carry JIFFY products.

"JIFFY brand muffins and other baking mixes . . . were precursors of the entire convenience food industry and made Mabel Holmes wealthy," an article in the *Ann Arbor News* reported.

In 1930 the biscuit mix not only introduced a new product line to the family business, but also solved the

MABEL HOLMES.

problem of what to do with low-grade flour, explained Roy Ives. "The prime outlet before had been crackers, but the biscuit mix could be made by blending it into the self-rising biscuit flour. This is one example of the genius of the Holmes family."

At first it wasn't easy to sell such a revolutionary idea to the public. Housewives were hesitant to use the baking mixes, afraid that their reputations as bakers would suffer. "In fact, for years the Chelsea Milling Company had problems getting customer endorsements," June Robinson remembered. "Housewives might like the taste, cost, and convenience of our products and secretly stock them on their pantry shelves, but they

IN THE 1930S, JIFFY BISCUIT MIX PACKAGING WAS PRINTED IN TWO TONES OF BLUE AND FEATURED APPETIZING FULL-COLOR PHOTOS OF WHAT CONSUMERS COULD MAKE WITH THE PRODUCT. ALTHOUGH THE PACKAGE APPEARANCE HAS CHANGED SLIGHTLY, MABEL'S ORIGINAL RECIPES CAN STILL BE FOUND ON THE MODERN-DAY PACKAGE. THE EARLY BOXES, IN THE DAYS BEFORE AUTOMATION, WERE HAND-ASSEMBLED AND GLUED.

didn't want family members or neighbors knowing they were using shortcuts."

In spring 1933, the public's opinion changed with an endorsement of JIFFY Mix by the Copeland Service, Inc., of New York. The Copeland Service was a food- and drug-testing laboratory owned by Royal Copeland, who was a U.S. senator from New York. Copeland's spirited advocacy of reforms to the Food and Drug Administration's policies were increasingly placing him in the public spotlight, and eventually led to the enactment of new legislation in 1938. A homeopathic physician, Copeland was originally from Dexter, Michigan, and had married Howard's cousin Frances. He agreed to test the product for quality and purity. The endorsement came on March 13, 1933, from Copeland associate Ole Salthe, giving the product the validity it needed, and JIFFY sales soared:

We have submitted your product, JIFFY MIX, to careful laboratory examination as well as to practical baking tests, and are

The Chelsea Milling Company's second complex of grain towers under construction in the 1930s.

happy to report that we have found the product to be of excellent quality and that JIFFY MIX will make quickly delicious biscuits of a good color, fine texture, tender and tasty. It was also gratifying to find that your product is nature matured and not chemically bleached.

Respectfully,
Copeland Service, Inc.

In June 1935 a small text advertisement for JIFFY read:

For Better Strawberry Shortcakes
Use Jiffy Mix
Easy Delicious Economical
Chelsea Milling Co.

SENATOR ROYAL S. COPELAND.

W hen Veryl Hafley started working at the mill in the 1930s, JIFFY sales were in full swing. He and six women formed the packaging department; they wrapped the JIFFY boxes by hand. "We were like one big, happy family—and I mean happy," he remembered. "Mr. Holmes was the sole boss. We had no superintendent." In those days, women worked eight-hour shifts and men worked twelve-hour shifts, from 6 a.m. to 6 p.m. The night shift never worked Saturdays, but the men on the day shifts reported for duty on Saturday mornings to clean the plant. Hafley usually worked Sundays as well. "We never shut anything down; we kept going."

As JIFFY production increased and space at the mill became a major concern, the April 7, 1934, edition of the *Ann Arbor News* announced that construction was about to begin on six storage tanks 120 feet in height (twenty feet taller than the three existing tanks). The new tanks would more than triple the mill's storage capacity to 160,000 bushels of grain. The paper announced that fifty local men would be hired as laborers, and the tanks would be made of concrete with steel reinforcement and without joints. "Forms for all the tanks will be poured continuously, nights, days, and Sundays, until the work is finished," the article noted. The writer added that each year the mill ground more than a half-million bushels of wheat and that the mill's flours are "marketed in New York City in more than 200 stores, as well as the middle west, New England states and the southwest, with Detroit providing the principal market."

At the pace business was growing, Howard Holmes was always alert to the need for future expansion space. As nearby houses went on the market, the Chelsea Milling Company quickly purchased the properties. One property right next to the mill required especially sensitive negotiations. A dilapidated house and outbuildings were nestled just beneath the tall white grain-storage tanks. Howard Holmes approached the owner, who repeatedly refused to sell. The house and other tumbledown buildings were all she had left of her husband's work, the owner explained. Finally Howard convinced her to sell, promising that he would install modern plumbing, mow the lawn, and allow her to continue to live there. She agreed. But when workmen tried to put an old woodshed out of its misery, the tearful elderly lady came to the mill owner, explaining that her deceased husband had built that shed long ago. Howard let the rickety woodshed stay.

Artist Jonathan Taylor captured the old house and its grounds in a pen-and-ink sketch of the mill.

Artist Jonathan Taylor captured the old house and its grounds in a pen-and-ink sketch of the mill. Intrigued by the mill when he drove through town, Taylor chose the Chelsea Milling Company silos as the model for the drawing he titled "American Cathedral," which pays tribute to the essential role that mills in general, and this mill in particular, played in the lives of generations of Americans. The original drawing hangs in the Smithsonian in Washington D.C., and a copy is in the Chelsea Milling Company's corporate boardroom.

THE CHELSEA MILLING COMPANY DEPICTED IN JONATHAN TAYLOR'S PEN-AND-INK
SKETCH "AMERICAN CATHEDRAL."

TRAGEDY STRIKES

The Twins Take Charge

HOWARD SUMNER HOLMES
1931

DUDLEY KIRKE HOLMES
1931

On October 29, 1936, tragedy hit the Holmes family when fifty-year-old Howard Samuel Holmes fell more than seventy feet to his death inside one of the Chelsea Milling Company's grain elevators.

"Milling was—and still can be—a profession fraught with danger," Dudley Holmes Sr. explained many years later. "Several times a year we would hear of someone crushed in machinery or slipping and falling in a grain elevator, then being suffocated to death. We had hoped it would never happen here."

Veryl Hafley was in the plant on that day. "I didn't know Mr. Holmes well, but I knew that he was for the people. He was the one that had kept everyone working during the Depression and we were all grateful." Bob Howe was also at the mill on October 29. "I remember that day as if it

were yesterday," he recalled. "The night before he died, Mr. Holmes had talked to me about the new equipment we were installing for pancake flour. He said, 'Bob, right now we're going to start making some money.' He was all worked up about that new equipment."

Howe explained how the accident might have happened. "We had to check the wheat in the elevators all the time because with too much moisture, it would start caking. You had to go all the way to the top of the tank to measure the moisture level. To check it out, we used a little platform rigged onto a cable. When you pushed the lever the cable tightened, and up went the man lift with you standing on it. When you got to the top, you hit a reverse arm; if you kept pushing on it, it would automatically start back down. There was no brake. Evidently, when Mr. Holmes got to the top of the silo, he held onto the man lift lever too long and it started reversing itself. That's when he fell."

Roy Ives's father, Wirt, found Howard at the bottom of the elevator, when he tripped over the crushed body.

The police asked twenty-three-year-old Dudley to identify his father's body. Afterward, he hurried over to East Middle Street to break the news to his mother. He brought Mabel's closest friend with him to comfort her, then drove to the University of Michigan to find his brother.

The story is now a classic in the Holmes family: how Dudley went from office to office on campus to find his brother, eventually interrupting an engineering professor. He dragged Howard out of class

71

CHELSEA MILLING FROM THE NORTHWEST CORNER LOOKING EAST. HOWARD SAMUEL HOLMES FELL TO HIS DEATH INSIDE ONE OF THESE GRAIN STORAGE TANKS.

and on the drive to Chelsea told him of their father's death.

"That one day, October 29, 1936, had a bearing on quite a lot of things . . . on many, many things," Dudley Sr. recalled with tears in his eyes sixty-six years later. "I can't classify the disease he had, but he had been suffering from an illness. He was not well. Sometimes he had the inability to stand up and go about work as he wanted to do. Unexpectedly he would have some sort of attack. There were rumors at his death, but Howard and I didn't put stock in any of the rumors. He was a sick man. Period."

Roy Ives remembered the senior Howard Holmes telling him once that he was a candidate for pernicious anemia—which is the illness that had taken Howard's father, Harmon Holmes. Perhaps that indirectly caused the accident, he speculated. But, no matter what the cause, Ives had warm memories of his first employer. "Mr. Holmes was a godsend to me when I was a high school senior in 1927 and 1928," recalled

THE CHELSEA MILLING CREW ON A SUMMER DAY IN THE 1930S. WIRT IVES (FRONT ROW,
FAR LEFT) WAS THE FIRST TO DISCOVER HOWARD SAMUEL HOLMES'S BODY AT THE
BOTTOM OF THE ELEVATOR SHAFT.

Ives. "When my father became desperately ill, there was no health or
disability insurance and our family had no income. Mr. Holmes hired
me to run the feed packers, and I packed bran and middlings into one-
hundred-pound sacks three nights a week, all night, and two nights until
midnight, so I could graduate with my class and thereby earn the living
for our family. I am eternally grateful to Mr. Holmes."

Mr. Holmes captained the enter-prise (Chelsea Milling Company) from small beginnings and devoted his time and thoughts whole-heartedly to it. During the period of the National Recovery Act, he served as regional representative for the National Flour Milling organization, assisting in formulating codes for this industry.

During the time Howard Samuel Holmes was engaged in bank-ing…he also continued other interests of his father, assuming charge of holdings that came to him by inheritance and enlarging them through application of his own special genius.

Mr. Holmes also concerned himself with civic affairs. A staunch Republican, he held, at various times, practically every office in Chelsea, yet he was in no sense a politician. Accepting public office only so that he might be of service to his fellow-citizens, he became a member of the Board of Education of Chelsea. Even when he was himself a student, he became interested in general educational af-fairs. As a recognition of his services to the University of Michigan, he was elected alumni president of the class of 1907 for a five-year term…Through it all, he always remained "Howdy."

Known for love of his community, Mr. Holmes, in the opinion of many who knew him best, did more for its welfare and progress than did any other man…

HOWARD SAMUEL HOLMES IN THE 1920S.

AFTER HER HUSBAND'S DEATH, MABEL HOLMES TOOK OVER MANAGEMENT OF THE CHELSEA
MILLING COMPANY, ASSISTED BY HER SONS. "MABEL WAS A GOOD BUSINESSPERSON—SHE HAD
A GOOD HEAD FOR FIGURES," DUDLEY (LEFT) RECALLED MANY YEARS LATER.

Howard's obituary in the *Chelsea Standard-Herald* reported details
about the accident and identified surviving members of the family:

> *Hundreds of Chelsea citizens and friends from many other
> Michigan and out-of-state cities were present at the funeral services
> held Sunday afternoon to pay their respects to Howard S. Holmes, who
> was instantly killed in a fall at the Chelsea Milling Company. . . .*
>
> *Services were held at the Holmes home on East Middle Street,
> where tribute was paid to the man who had been a lifelong resident
> of the community, was the friend of everyone with whom he came in
> contact, either in a business way or through social connections, and
> who was highly respected as a leading citizen, as a progressive business
> man and as a benefactor of all worthy causes within the community. . . .*
>
> *Mr. Holmes was instantly killed about 9:30 Tuesday forenoon,
> October 29, 1936, when he fell 70 feet down a passenger elevator shaft*

of a grain storage tank at the mill. Finding that one of the storage tanks had been overheating, he had gone to the top of the tower to read a meter, but what caused him to fall from the elevator has not been determined. Wirt Ives, a workman at the mill, found his body. . . .

He is survived by the widow, twin sons, Howard, a student in the University of Michigan, and Dudley, who has been working at the milling company with his father; a brother, Ralph H. Holmes of Battle Creek; and a sister, Enid P. Ellis of Grand Rapids. . . .

After Howard's death, the Chelsea State Bank passed a resolution about its former director, noting:

He took an active interest in his community and was always willing to lend his assistance, both financially and otherwise, to the affairs of his community in order to make it a better place in which to live and to assist those who were less fortunate than himself.

Howard S. Holmes needs the testimony of no man in his favor. The things he did and the life he led are our strongest consolation now that he has gone. Perhaps it is enough to say of him, that his life and works constitute his best eulogy.

His fraternity, Sigma Alpha Epsilon, added: "He was the quietest, most self-effacing person in the chapter. But he was always cool, and sure of himself, and completely competent."

When the funeral service was over, the mill continued just as it had. Mabel and the The Boys had recognized the importance of keeping the mill wheels turning in the wake of the tragedy. "We were shocked, but the place kept running," Bob Howe said. "That's when The Boys took over. They kept things going just about the same as they had been."

Howard's death propelled his wife, Mabel, into the presidency of the company, with Howard and Dudley taking on administrative roles. Years later Mabel White Holmes was nominated for the Michigan Women's Hall of Fame by Lucille Williams, a teacher and family friend who noted, "As a businesswoman, Mabel excelled, not by choice, but by necessity. . . . Qualities of character in this remarkable woman still permeate the

Chelsea Milling Company, where some employees have been working for as long as forty-five years. Thoughtfulness, kindness, respect for women's rights, as well as for those of men, are the rule. Would that all women could leave as great a legacy!"

Dudley had finished his degree at the University of Michigan the summer before his father died. Howard had transferred from Princeton to Michigan in order to study engineering. He was still a year away from graduation but decided to take a year off from school to help his brother run the plant. Howard then returned to the University of Michigan to finish his degree. It was there that he met his future wife, Tiny, on a blind date. The two dated steadily over the next six years.

Mabel served as president until 1940, when she became a member of the mill's board of directors. She continued to hold an interest in the family business until her death in 1977. "Mabel was a very efficient and very involved participant in the day-to-day running of the business," her son Dudley recalled. "She was a good businessperson. She had a good head for figures. If she were alive today, she would be at the head of some large corporation; she was that good at business. Her baking mixes were her pride and joy. I know my father was always confident that if anything happened to him, she would be able to handle the business and all it entailed."

"Qualities of character in this remarkable woman still permeate the Chelsea Milling Company. . . . Thoughtfulness, kindness, respect for women's rights, as well as for those of men, are the rule."

"This is one man's opinion, but I think Mabel was responsible for much of the success in establishing the mill's role in the future," said Chelsea attorney John Keusch. "She was quite a gal."

WHEN MABEL HOLMES WAS NOMINATED TO THE MICHIGAN WOMEN'S HALL OF FAME, THE PROGRAM NOTED, "AS A BUSINESSWOMAN, MABEL EXCELLED, NOT BY CHOICE, BUT BY NECESSITY."

THE SECOND HOWARD HOLMES IN THE EARLY 1930S.

THE THIRD GENERATION
Howard and Dudley Find Their Footing

"We knew right away that October 29, 1936, would change everything in our lives," Dudley Holmes Sr. said many years later. "Still, Howard and I had both been interested in the milling company. We grew up in and around the mill, doing the various little chores that people could entrust to kids our ages. I can't remember a time when my life didn't center around the mill. When you're third generation, it's just a part of you. I wouldn't say we were ready to head the business in 1936, but we did the best we could."

"Howard hadn't planned on coming to the mill to work after graduation," his wife, Tiny, said. "He had accepted a job with an engineering firm in Chicago, but when his father died, he decided that his place was at the mill. He never said that he was disappointed he couldn't do what he'd intended to do. He did what he felt was the right thing to do." When corporate administrator Sandy Schultz cleaned out Howard's office after his death, she found a stack of letters from companies like Procter & Gamble and Westinghouse dated 1937, each containing job offers. "He had kept those letters all his life," she said.

After their father's death, the first decision the two brothers made was to make as few changes as possible. "When they went to work at the mill, they felt they had to act like they knew what they were doing, for the sake of the employees," said Tiny Holmes. "We were smart enough to recognize the talent of the people that my father had in place, and we let them continue to do what they did best," recalled Dudley Sr.

At Mabel's suggestion, a part-time manager, Clarence Athanson, was hired to help her run the company. From 1940 on, Mabel maintained an office at the mill and served on the board of directors. Howard supervised sales and administration and relied on his engineering background to oversee the maintenance and design of equipment. Dudley became secretary-treasurer. He secured the raw materials for the package mixes, managed the flour mill, and over time developed seventeen new products. "There is so much to this grain business. It worked well to share the management," recalled Dudley.

Business in the mid-twentieth century was very different from business in the early twenty-first century. "Life was simple then," Tiny recalled. People walked instead of driving. Each day Howard would walk samples over to the house on East Middle Street for Dudley's wife, Nancy, to test bake. Even forms of communication were quite different from what they are today. If the twins needed to conduct business by phone, Howard or Dudley would have to walk downtown to the telephone office, which was on the second floor of what is now Chelsea Market. "The switchboard looked like something out of a Lily Tomlin skit," June Robinson remembered. "In the 1940s, there was no air conditioning, so the windows would all be open. If the operators saw Dudley or Howard out on the street, they would holler out the window, 'Mr. Holmes! You've got a call from Boston!' Then he would climb the stairs and take the call. Our phone number here at the mill was 20."

Even the rodent control was different in those days. One could say it was "all natural." The Holmes family happily welcomed cats into the mill to keep the rodent population down.

Even the rodent control was different in those days. One could say it was "all natural." The Holmes family happily welcomed cats into the mill to keep the rodent population down. "You had to love animals if you worked for Howard and Dudley," said June Robinson. "When we fumigated, we'd close the plant down, round up the bunch of cats, put them in a boxcar with a dish of milk for each one, and they would stay there for the weekend."

Other four-legged creatures were welcome at the mill too. Howard's dog, an English springer spaniel named Duffy, accompanied him to the mill every day. "He was like a member of the family," Robinson said. "Duffy would cross the railroad tracks and visit the local businessmen on Main Street every day; he knew every butcher in town and they knew him. He often returned with bones." Robinson lived in the country, and she would occassionally take Duffy home with her so he could romp and play.

THE FIRST DECISION THE BROTHERS MADE IN 1936 WAS TO MAKE AS FEW
CHANGES AS POSSIBLE.

B eing hands-on managers throughout most of their lives, The Boys would always fill in where help was needed. During business hours, the brothers wore suits and handled the corporate side of the business. At night and on weekends, they dressed in overalls and hauled 100-pound bags of flour, swept the loading docks, and answered mail. In Dudley's words, "We had the privilege of doing the whole damn thing ourselves. The men in the different departments taught us what to do."

As often as he could, Howard would go on the road, trying to introduce the JIFFY business to other markets in the Midwest and Pennsylvania. Many weeks, Howard would be gone all week and Dudley would supervise the mill; then the brothers would work together in the mill all weekend. Often Howard would arrive as early as three in the morning. "Everyone in town knew that Howard was a workaholic. The mill became his life," said Lynwood Noah, Howard's childhood friend.

The brothers shared the work by focusing on their areas of interest and abilities. Howard took an active interest in the design and maintenance of the machinery. "Howard loved engineering and machinery," Tiny Holmes, said. "At some point before his father died, Howard had taken time off from school to work on developing a hydrogen engine that ran on water," she recalled. "I don't know all the specifics, just that it was an ambitious undertaking." Dudley had a strong interest in commodities brokering and applied that to his work at the mill.

Howard's and Dudley's personalities helped to maintain the same commitment to a family atmosphere that had characterized the mill from its early days. Right up until World War II, the number of employees was never larger than thirty, and everyone knew not only each other's name but also the names of everyone's wife, husband, and children—and a great deal about their personal lives too. One employee who couldn't read was too proud to tell anyone, but he would bring his mail to Dudley and ask him to read it aloud, explaining, "I forgot my glasses." Dudley never let on that he knew differently.

At the start of World War II, the War Department informed the owners of the Chelsea Milling Company that one of the twins— but not both—could be given a military deferment. "In April 1943, my father took the decision into his own hands," Dudley Jr. said. "One day he came home and told my mother that he had enlisted and would be leaving in two days. That was that."

Dudley Sr. explained a half century later. "I enlisted in the navy almost immediately after we heard about Pearl Harbor. Nancy and I had been married a short time then."

George Staffan of Staffan Funeral Home in Chelsea remembered driving to the Army Recruiting Center with Howard shortly after Dudley's enlistment. "We were the only two to get a deferment that day," he said. "Howard got his deferment on account of the business he was in—food was essential to the war effort—and I was working with the health department, both in Chelsea and Ann Arbor. The other embalmer had gone to war, so I got a deferment."

Dudley Sr. was sent to the South Pacific along with several of his employees at the Chelsea Milling Company. Assigned to ships carrying supplies, he saw ferocious fighting on the islands. Eventually he landed

One son went to war and the other stayed on at the mill. Dudley enlisted soon after Pearl Harbor, while Howard obtained a deferment. On a brief visit home, Dudley posed with (left to right) his daughter Diane; his mother, Mabel; Mabel's sister, Estelle; his wife, Nancy; Howard's future wife, Mary (Tiny); and the family dog, Duffy.

on Ie Shima (shima means "island"), where he served as an escort to journalist Ernie Pyle on the day before Pyle was killed. "Ie Shima was a beautiful little island, not more than six or seven miles long, next to Okinawa. It was quite a famous place in those days, with a little mountain in the center," remembered Dudley Sr. "We had pretty good underground structures for protection when the bombs flew, and we had enough brains to use them." When he heard that Ernie Pyle had been killed, he was shocked. "I can remember being so d—d mad that I could have taken on his assailants bare-handed. It was a terrible loss. He was a fine writer and gentleman."

To coordinate the war effort, the federal government imposed new rules and regulations on mills all across America. "Two government men in white coats would come every day and have us grind their flour," remembered employee Corky Palmer. "The flour was pure black. It was distributed all over the world." The flour "wasn't the pure white that we were used to," explained Tiny Holmes, "because the government wanted it in great bulk and in a hurry, so it was ground with bran—and probably middlings—in it."

Because so many able-bodied men were in the military and the mill was operating day and night, Howard had to find workers wherever he could. Palmer recalled working alongside gandy dancers from the railroad, who would punch time cards whenever their shifts allowed. During and immediately after the war, raw materials were scarce and often rationed, which meant that Chelsea Milling could make only limited amounts of JIFFY products. Because gasoline was also rationed, Howard had to do most of his selling by phone rather than by car. He sold JIFFY products to a few established customers, explained food broker and friend Wendell Kofler. "In 1945 Howard Holmes was the entire sales department for the company. He would make as much product as he could," said Kofler, "and then try to get distribution in markets close to Michigan. He would pick one or two customers he wanted long-term, and that's where he would make his allocations."

Dudley had married his wife, Nancy, in 1941, before his enlistment. Back on the home front, Howard and Mary (Tiny) Blodgett decided to tie the knot in 1945. "I've always been associated with identical twins," said Tiny. "My brothers were identical twins, and then I married an identical twin. I've seen firsthand that it's hard to be identical—you tend not to

have an identity until you get separated."

When the war ended, Dudley Sr. took some time away from the family to find his own identity and to reacclimate himself to civilian life. For sixteen or seventeen months he worked as a commodities broker, first in Chicago and then in Detroit. In the end, he chose to return to the family business. This forced him and his brother to face the task of dividing the responsibilities that Howard had handled by himself. "They decided that for one year Howard would take sales and Dudley would run the plant, then the next year they'd switch," recalled Harry Kealy, who worked at Chelsea Milling for forty years. Before twelve months ended, however, the brothers realized that their plan wouldn't work. "Howard had charisma and could handle people; Dudley was good at buying raw materials," said Kealy. "They also realized their positions needed continuity. They couldn't keep swapping jobs. They needed to keep things the way they were."

At the end of the war, the *Ann Arbor News* ran a photograph of the Chelsea Milling Company and its silos with the caption:

> *To the distressed of Europe, (the silos) might be a reflection of American sympathy and helpfulness. From this mill flows a steady stream of flour for Europe's bread. For American consumers there is also a huge output of not only flour but also prepared mixes for the home baking. . . . Howard and Dudley Holmes, twin brothers, and their mother, Mrs. Howard Holmes, with 40 employees, operate this mill.*

POSTWAR BOOM
Momentum Gathers with Changing Sales Strategies

T hroughout the history of the Chelsea Milling Company, JIFFY
sales have been pretty accurate indicators of the health of the
national economy—and vice versa. "If the economy was down,
we did great, because housewives were looking for bargains and
shopping carefully," pointed out employee Mike Sweet. "If the economy
was good, our business would drop a bit, as consumers experimented
with high-priced brands and families ate out more."

"The business survived because it offered products that made life more convenient for women," said Tiny Holmes. "It continued to survive because more women went to work and were released from the kitchens. They looked for shortcuts to help them feed their families and get a meal together faster and better," she said. "Today, JIFFY is still a convenience. In fact, Mabel's original intent became a reality—even a man can do it!"

"The success of this business rested on cooperation, having everyone work together to make the business succeed," said June Robinson. "It also rested on the fact that we made good products and sold them for a good price. Yet another reason for success was the fact that we had very fine people to work with—I don't say *for*, but *with*."

"You had to be a good, hard worker because those boys knew how to work," recalled Harry Kealy. "A lot of times Dudley or Howard would call me to come over on a Sunday morning, and I would throw down 100-pound bags into a railroad car alongside them. They weren't afraid to work."

Nancy and Tiny worked side by side with their husbands to fill in where needed. They both prepared and tested JIFFY products. When Tiny and Howard were first married, they worked together at the mill on weekends. "We'd all go down to the plant and package mixes," Tiny said. "I'd dump the mix into the boxes. Another person would weigh them on the scale. Then the top would be glued in place, and off the boxes would go on a forklift. This was a family business, and there is an extra complexity in living and working in that situation."

When a new doughnut mix was added to the product line, Tiny would get up early in the morning before Howard left for his road trips to deep-fry fresh doughnuts for him to take as samples. "Ugh! I did not enjoy smelling hot fat first thing in the morning!" she recalled

TINY HOLMES WOULD RISE EARLY IN THE MORNING WHEN HOWARD WAS TRAVELING AND BAKE FRESH DOUGHNUTS FOR HIM TO TAKE ALONG AS SAMPLES.

with a smile and a shudder. "That's the only product I was ever directly involved with. After that time I didn't have anything much to do with the business other than making Howard available. He was a very hard-working man. I was kept busy raising five children."

The family attracted hard-working employees as well. Glenn Lehr, head of sales for the company, would often arrive at the office around 5 a.m., push hard through the day, then occasionally "take five," June Robinson recalled. "He would lie right down on the floor and nap for five minutes, though you'd think he'd had eight hours of sleep when he got up. He just kept on going. He was a lot like Howard in that regard, which is why they worked together so well."

Lehr's first day at work set the tone for his career at Chelsea Milling. He was hired the day after he met Howard. Early in the morning of his first day at work, he asked Howard to tell him the company's most pressing problem. "We have a lot of them," said Howard, "but right now there's a problem with bug infestation in a warehouse in Richmond." Lehr offered to fly to Virginia. Howard called for flight information and was told that the next plane left in an hour and a half. The two men raced to the plane. "Everything happened so fast that I didn't even

JIFFY SALES PICKED UP QUICKLY WHEN WORLD WAR II RATIONING ENDED, AND HOWARD WAS ABLE TO RETURN TO THE ROAD TO MAKE SALES CALLS.

know the price of the products yet," recalled Lehr. After dealing with the Richmond problem, the two flew to Winston-Salem, North Carolina, cleaned up those warehouses, destroyed infested product, and only *then* sat down to discuss what they were going to do together.

"That year, 1946, saw very little business, but we were in a position to meet the competition—which was formidable," Lehr recalled. "The war had just ended. We had hot roll mix, bread mix, doughnut mix, pie crust mix, and baking mix—which we called 'biscuit mix' back then. We had nothing much in the line of salesmen or customers, but we were up against some powerhouses in the industry. Duncan Hines had 247 people out there; Chelsea Milling had Howard and me."

Howard had several options. He could hire salesmen to visit customers, which was an expensive option, or he could use food brokers in markets where he wanted to increase distribution. He decided to retain Wendell Kofler as the company's first sales representative. Lehr,

Kofler, and Howard all acknowledged that marketing would be their first challenge. Lehr suggested that the company focus on having the best-quality product at the best price. He also suggested that twice a year Chelsea Milling should introduce a "shocker price" that would take the place of a national advertising program. "That decision started out as a conservative philosophy, but over the years it became revolutionary, as competitors dedicated huge budgets to advertising and promotions," said Kofler. "Only once did we experiment with advertisements. That was for the doughnut mix. We found that ads didn't pull any business and we decided to abandon advertising. Instead, Chelsea Milling would make the best product at the lowest and best price."

Consumers could count on JIFFY for great taste and convenience. Kofler could count on JIFFY to get the products where they needed to be when they needed to be there, he said. "Chelsea Milling drivers were very unusual people who demonstrated the loyalty that ran all through the company," he recalled. "When an order was taken, I never had to use the phrase 'sometime this week' when I talked about a delivery date. I knew precisely when those deliveries would be made. Super Foods, our biggest customer, would open to accept deliveries at seven a.m., and the JIFFY truck would be there waiting. They could set their clock by JIFFY's punctuality. That made selling easier."

> *To make certain that stores didn't buy JIFFY on sale and then raise the price, Howard decided to have the price printed right on the boxes.*

In 1946, when Kofler's firm was asked to sell JIFFY products, Glenn Lehr asked Howard if Chelsea Milling could manufacture a hot roll mix, doughnut mix, and bread mix that would each sell for a dime. A pie crust mix had been introduced in 1940. Howard took out the slide rule that accompanied him everywhere, made his calculations, and said it could be done. The dime price was the first "shocker" price, and it worked. Howard ran several "shocker" sales each year with the stipulation that the savings were passed along to the consumers. To make certain that stores didn't buy JIFFY on sale and then raise the price, Howard decided to have the price printed right on the boxes. Harry Kealy took the pie

JIFFY PRODUCTS BECAME STAPLES IN MANY KITCHENS DURING THE 1950S. EARLY BOXES WERE ROBIN'S EGG BLUE. THE TRADEMARK BLUE AND WHITE BOXES WERE FIRST INTRODUCED IN 1961.

THIS DRAMATIC PICTURE OF THE TOWERS WAS TAKEN IN 1959, FACING THE NORTHWEST, LOOKING AT THE SOUTH AND EAST SIDES OF THE MILL.

crust cartons—all 48,000 of them—on a skid to the *Chelsea Standard*, where the newspaper's printers stamped "10 cents" on them, and then Kealy loaded everything back on the truck and brought the boxes back to be packaged and sold.

"The company didn't go national right away," said Kofler. "In 1947 Howard started signing up brokers, but they were confined to the Midwest to start with. The company's growth was gradual. I would say that it took ten years for JIFFY mixes to become available nationally."

Local consumers could still walk over to Chelsea Milling and purchase flour at the sales window. The mill still produced Phoenix flour for grocery company C. F. Smith, sold wheat germ to health food companies, bran to Kellogg's, and middlings to companies producing animal feed. Soon, however, JIFFY sales began to soar, and the increased demand for JIFFY meant that Chelsea Milling needed all the flour the mill could process. Sales of flour ended in the mid-1960s.

Although Chelsea Milling would hire only a half-dozen or so people a year immediately after the war, hundreds of people would apply, recalled Cal Summers, who worked there for forty-two years. "I

RAW MATERIALS ARRIVED FROM THE WEST BY TRAIN. TRAINS ALSO CARRIED JIFFY PRODUCTS FROM CHELSEA TO LOCATIONS AROUND THE NATION.

remember Howard figured out that the fairest thing to do would be to number the applications, and after twenty or so we wouldn't take any more. The people were hired in order, no matter who it was. That didn't work too good, but Howard was trying to be fair."

But the company soon expanded its workforce. In 1952, forty people worked for Chelsea Milling. Within six years the number had tripled, and flour sales now accounted for only 20 percent of the company's revenue. By the 1960s, about 180 employees were working around the clock during the busy months of the year, and the number of prepared mixes had grown to seventeen (the last products added were fudge and spice brownies and two frostings). That year, for the first time, JIFFY products could be purchased in all fifty states, including the newest state, Hawaii.

OUTSIDE THE BOX

Chelsea Milling Innovates and Automates

HOWARD IN FRONT OF CHELSEA MILLING'S GRAIN TOWERS. THE COMPANY BECAME KNOWN AS THE "LITTLE GIANT" OF THE PREPARED-MIX INDUSTRY DURING THE POST-WORLD WAR II YEARS. JOURNALISTS FLOCKED TO CHELSEA TO SEE JIFFY'S REVOLUTIONARY CONVEYANCE SYSTEM AND PRODUCTION LINES.

Business became increasingly exciting for Howard and Dudley following the war, spurred by the end of wartime rationing, by breakthroughs in automation technologies, and by a competitive convenience food industry. As returning veterans married, settled down, and started having families, JIFFY sales began to skyrocket.

In 1952, Howard reported that JIFFY's ready-mix products ranked between first and third in national sales. The plant had recently installed ten long lines of automatic packaging machinery, and roller conveyors now replaced forklift skids in the warehouse. Howard's warehousing approach was unique in the whole milling industry.

Roy Ives, the second generation of his family to work at the mill, noted that the Chelsea Milling Company was the first in the nation to have a practical application for computer-controlled packaging and shipping lines. "This small company in a small town in Michigan couldn't be capsized by the milling giants," he said proudly. "They were competitive world-wide." A December 15, 1956, *Ann Arbor News* article echoed those sentiments. Under the headline "Automation, Product Variations Spark Milling Output," the story made the point that automation and dry package mixes were infusing new life into an age-old industry. Howard was quoted as calling JIFFY products "the sparkplug to company sales." At that time, the product line consisted of biscuit, corn muffin, doughnut, pie crust, and pancake mixes, as well as frostings and four flavors of cake mix. The reporter explained how the innovative Chelsea Milling system worked:

> *The ready mix materials are automatically funneled into the packages along a moving conveyor belt. They are weighed automatically. The packages—boxes with inner protective lining—are folded automatically, prior to receiving the material. They are closed automatically.*
>
> *The boxes move along the line into the shipping department. This department, also used as a warehouse, is being completely mechanized. The product eventually will be stored in designated spaces without human hands touching even the boxes.*

The Chelsea Milling Company was the first in the world to have a complete conveyance system, which initially was more than twenty miles in length. Businessmen and engineers from around the world flew into Detroit and then drove out to rural Chelsea to see the extraordinary system in operation. "Still, they never did get all the kinks out of the automated system," Harry Kealy remembered. "A man by the name of Kevin would sit and watch a monitor for hours to make sure it was working right. Nine different lines sent product onto this big belt."

Renovations continued in the early 1960s, when the company

dismantled an old 350-barrel-a-day mill and built a new milling tower capable of producing 2,000 barrels of flour a day, an amount that would soon be needed, given the expansion of the JIFFY business. After that, Chelsea Milling could produce more packages during one hour than either Pillsbury or General Mills could in any of their plants. That production increase gave Chelsea Milling a major advantage because of its ability to cut prices. "Howard would run a special on biscuit mix, and those two big companies would call and tell him to get it off the market because it was hurting them," said Kealy. "They were competitors, but they always got along well together."

Howard designed and constructed a "very, very ingenious warehouse," recalled Donald M. Mennel, owner of Mennel Milling Company in Fostoria, Ohio. "It was really famous in its day. I call it the 'Roller Skate Warehouse.'" Roller skate conveyors carried the product all the way to the loading area. Howard also installed electronically

ON THE CUTTING EDGE OF AUTOMATION, HOWARD INTRODUCED MANY TIME-SAVING MACHINES AND PRODUCTION METHODS. THE CHELSEA MILLING COMPANY WAS THE FIST AMERICAN FIRM TO INTRODUCE COMPUTER-CONTROLLED PACKAGING AND TRANSPORT LINES.

controlled equipment with a sorting system that segregated products and an electronic memory circuit that could precisely fill orders. "This was revolutionary for its time," said Mennel. "The trade magazines all wrote articles about it. Howard's warehouse system was the forerunner of today's computerized warehouse. Howard was trained as an engineer, and that explains why such a sophisticated system could be found first in such a small company."

During the same period, Dudley designed an advanced test kitchen in the plant. "Eventually, the scales we used were so sensitive that they could detect the difference between two and three grains of sugar," he said. "The mixes had to be done exactly." Dudley was also in charge of plant operations, which included managing the grain supply and ordering the tremendous quantities of sugar, cocoa, baking powder, lard, and flavorings necessary for the mixes. "Those were good days. Busy days. Exciting days," he remembered. "There was always something happening."

"Look at what 25 cents buys—two boxes of JIFFY Pie Crust Mix!"

An Eye on the Bottom Line
Passing on the Savings to Consumers

T he Holmes brothers were generous people privately, but their company expenditures were made very carefully and as seldom as possible. "I can never remember buying anything new," said Howard's secretary, June Robinson. Heat was scarce in the old offices in winter, so Robinson brought a little electric heater to work. Howard, who would often come to his office at three or four in the morning, would borrow her heater until she arrived. "He never splurged and bought himself a heater, and when mine wore out he had one of our machinists fix it up. We never threw anything away," she recalled.

Like many others, Harry Kealy did anything that needed doing. Besides supervising the loading, shipping, and receiving department, he would drive a truck when drivers called in sick, shop around for deals when parts or office supplies were needed, or tinker with a machine that was giving them trouble. "Harry had a way of finding the best deal on whatever it was we needed," Dudley Jr. said.

The mill's policy of carefully considering all capital expenditures meant that employees were often asked to be creative. Rather than buying new equipment, the mill often purchased older models and fixed or altered the machinery. "In the plant, we used a lot of Kellogg's cast-offs," Robinson recalled. "Walter Scott would take that old machinery and convert it into working condition for our needs. Those machines would just keep on going, and every week we would have to make out orders for parts," said Veryl Hafley. "We had to solve all the problems ourselves. There was no electrician on staff in the early days. Duane 'Drano' Walz was the master of the frosting equipment. The cylinder of that machine never worked right. After an hour or two, it would clog up and Duane would have to come and tear it apart." Once, a box maker was purchased from General Mills, Harry Kealy remembered. "It was designed to make bigger boxes, so our mechanics redid it. The boys in the tool room could do anything."

In the 1960s, Howard started taking Wayne Ruggles on trips to consider machinery purchases. At one time, Royal Pudding offered to sell a machine that had cost $300,000 new, but it was filthy. Howard looked at it, called it a "piece of junk," and was ready to leave, but Ruggles convinced him to pay $500 for the machine. He cleaned it up, and it is still running today—Number 12. "Howard definitely got his money's worth from that purchase—many times over," said Ruggles. Eventually, he convinced Howard to open a machine shop to make the necessary parts for repairs on site, and he credited Dudley Jr. with equipping and supporting the tool room and machine shop. "I appreciate the time he took with us," Ruggles said. "Once, Dudley Jr. pretty much wrote me a blank check and said, 'Anything you need, you get.' He understood that in the long run, the investment would be paid back many times over."

Ruggles kept careful records of the parts his crew made and how much they saved the company. "In our highest year, I could prove that we saved the company $750,000," he said. "I suggested to Howard that he keep my pay and give me ten percent of what I saved him, but he just laughed."

"That's how we got things done—as economically as we could," June Robinson recalled. "That was a reflection of the Depression and the time when we grew up."

Transportation in those days was a huge expense that required constant vigilance. Everything was loaded onto railcars by hand. The shipping agent for the railroad was also the local telegraph operator and ticket agent. Chelsea's station agent, Bob Devine, came to Chelsea in 1947 as one of the highest-paid agents on the Michigan Central line—"probably because of the Chelsea Milling business," he speculated. "I had it good here working with Howard, Dudley, Walter Scott, and Jess Meininger—and, of course, the boys in the warehouse. When I started here, we were what I would call a small company; ten or fifteen people worked in the office on bills of lading. It was so crowded in there that people were falling all over each other."

One important challenge was to locate good Class A boxcars qualified to transport flour. "A lot of them were in poor shape; many had been used to haul steel," Devine recalled. "One time we managed

to find a car to carry bran and sent it to the Midwest Biscuit Company. The car was refused there, and we got it back still full. I tested it, then tasted the bran. It tasted just like iodine." Flour quickly absorbs smells, and the railcar had been used earlier for an iodine shipment. To prevent the problem from happening again, Chelsea Milling began using covered hoppers specifically designated for flour and flour products. That worked well until one time when the supply of hoppers ran out. Customers were clamoring for their product, and the company was forced to substitute coal hoppers. "They put heavy plastic over them and loaded them with wheat," Devine said. "People were creative about getting their job done."

In the days before railroad deregulation, rail rates on flour and grain were complicated and difficult to determine; they were based on how much the company could load onto the cars. For the twenty-seven years Bob Devine supervised the railroad in Chelsea, Chelsea Milling was the biggest shipper in town. "My records show that Chelsea Milling

Laying the foundation for the new complex of grain towers in the mid-1960s, prior to the company's major sales surge in the 1970s.

was shipping up to seven hundred or eight hundred carloads of flour a year," Devine said. Each car could hold 50,000 pounds of flour; newer cars eventually could transport as much as 120,000 pounds. Devine soon discovered that Chelsea Milling's traffic manager, Clarence Athanson, was a rate specialist. "I used to spend a lot of time with him," he said. "Clarence had a lot of power. He knew the president of the railroad, and he wouldn't hesitate to go to him if there was trouble. Eventually, the railroad company became suspicious of our business relationship. They went so far as to have the ICC come investigate me." For three days, Interstate Commerce Commission experts studied Devine's books, all his accounts, even his personal bank account. "They couldn't find anything, of course," he said. "Clarence was just smarter than most people who were working for the railroad, and the railroad couldn't figure out how he could figure rates so well."

Keeping track of the railcars as they sped all over the country was a nightmarish and time-consuming job. When a customer called asking where his shipment was, Devine would have to phone the railroad office in Detroit and give the car number, destination, and route. Then that person would go to the next railroad to see if the company had a record of where the car was. The process would be repeated until the car could be tracked down. "Dudley Sr. would get on my neck about it," Devine said. "He would take matters in his own hands and call to trace a car. Somehow I always managed to call Dud back before the railroad did, and tell him the whereabouts. That would really start him off! There was always a family feeling here, and you felt like you were treated like one of them. Everybody worked together and we had a good time."

Howard was as careful about the consumer's dollar as he was about the company's dollar. He wanted to keep JIFFY prices as low as possible. "Howard felt that he was trying to do a service to the public, so he wouldn't raise the price unless he absolutely had to, in order to keep the company going," explained Tiny Holmes. It was a black week in the office if the mill ever had to raise prices, many old-timers remembered. Employee Delores Fouty pointed out that "Howard really hated to do that." Chelsea Milling went as many as eight years without a price increase—"unbelievable in this day and age."

Keeping the profit margin so tight meant that Chelsea Milling had no extra capital to lavish on advertising or public relations. Unlike its competitors, Chelsea Milling never employed an advertising or marketing firm. Staff members and administrators found creative and inexpensive ways to get the word out to consumers. Based on suggestions from JIFFY drivers, Howard had the delivery trucks painted in the trademark white and blue with JIFFY in huge letters. "Those served as traveling billboards for us," employee Dale Tripp recalled.

"From fixing equipment to designing packages and sending press releases, we did everything ourselves," June Robinson remembered.

CHELSEA WAS STILL A RURAL VILLAGE IN THE 1960S WHEN CHELSEA MILLING HAD JUST
COMPLETED A MAJOR ADDITION TO THE TOWER COMPLEX. BUSINESSMEN CAME FROM AROUND
THE WORLD TO SEE FIRSTHAND THE COMPANY'S INNOVATIVE CONVEYANCE SYSTEM.

"This is one of the reasons people can buy JIFFY mixes so cheaply."

In a file cabinet in Sandy Schultz's office is a very early prototype
for a JIFFY box. The second Howard's handwriting at the top of the box
lists the reasons for JIFFY's existence: "BISCUITS MADE IN A JIFFY:
No Fuss—No Bother—No Failures." At the bottom, Howard, with an
eye on the future, added another sales pitch: "Nature-Matured—NOT
Chemically Bleached."

"JIFFY"
baking mix
(BISCUIT)
NET WT. 40 OZ. (2½ LBS.)

Howard encouraged innovation, initiative, and creativity from everyone, not just his sales staff. June Robinson helped Phyllis Stepp develop cookbooks to promote JIFFY products by showing alternative uses for each mix. They were particularly proud of a corn cake recipe they developed. They gave JIFFY salesmen Presto griddles and taught them how to bake the corn cakes on the griddles so they could teach customers. "There were about twenty salesmen at the time, so we had twenty griddles plugged in at once," recalled Robinson. "Needless to say, our electrician was kept busy all that day, as we kept blowing the wiring!" Stepp and Robinson also designed the test kitchen from scratch and then went to Chelsea Lumber to choose the cupboards, which other employees installed. In that kitchen, the women taught the salesmen to bake cakes and biscuits, so they could demonstrate the products' convenience all over the country. "Some of those men worked a longtime before they got the hang of baking, but we wanted them to show our product at its best," remembered Robinson. "It was our idea that if you took hot baked goods into a company at coffee break time, it would be a cinch to get an order. And it worked!"

Pat Dittmar helped launch the JIFFY plant tour program, which has attracted as many as 2,500 visitors a month to Chelsea. Mill employees took the photographs of the plant that were used for the slide program. June Robinson worked on designing the baking mix package. She gathered a pretty glass candy jar from her desk, a basket, a blue napkin, and a pie plate from home. She and Howard flew to Chicago, where photographers placed strawberry shortcake on the pie plate and cookies in the jar. Then they started taking pictures. "That picture is still on the JIFFY boxes today, and I still have those things at home," said Robinson proudly. Rather than hire teams of product consultants, Dudley Sr., Howard, and staff members would take new products home to test on their families. They also distributed fresh baked goods to farmers waiting in line to deliver their wheat and to visitors waiting for the plant tour.

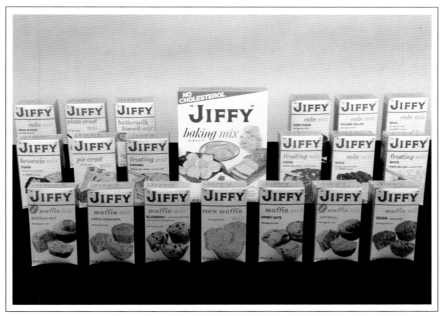

GROWING PAINS IN THE 1950s AND 1960s

Rising Sales and an Overseas Test Market

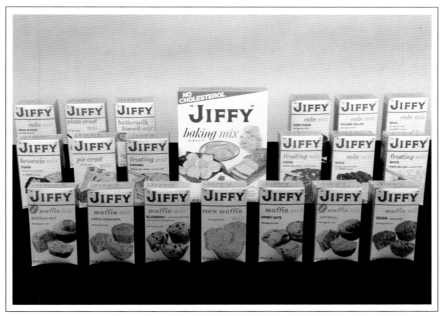

THE JIFFY PRODUCT LINE GREW DRAMATICALLY DURING THE 1950S AMD 1960S.

JIFFY sales grew consistently every year during Glenn Lehr's twenty-four years as head of sales. "As volume increased, Howard did everything he could think of to keep pace with production," Lehr said. "Meanwhile, I bought premiums for our buyers—golf clubs, fur coats, appliances. I'd seen that work in my days with General Mills."

Lehr spent nearly every weekday and some weekends on the road. The year after he arrived, the company started hiring brokers to expand their sales operation. When he left in 1970, the sales force had grown from two—Howard and Lehr—to eighty-two, including brokers.

"Howard and I formed a great relationship. I think I knew him as well as anybody," recalled Lehr. "Throughout the years, we spent many, many nights together in a hotel room battling the business. It was a battle. But he had both the personality and the technical knowledge to get a tremendous amount done."

Sales soared in the 1950s, when *Consumer Reports* announced that its staff had tested both JIFFY and Betty Crocker baking mixes and rated JIFFY higher. Howard mailed copies of that report to customers and potential customers all around the country. It was a real public relations boost for the company, more than one employee remembered.

Plant schedules and operations had to keep pace with sales growth. When William Cole was hired for the mixing crew in 1953, the company was producing baking mix, corn muffin mix, and pie crust mix. Production started in the fall and shut down in the spring. When the white cake mix was introduced, Willis Heydlauff ran the first batch for the employees; the second batch went to the public. Yellow cake was introduced shortly afterward. Production hours lengthened. Howard agreed to produce institutional mixes for prisons and schools; these would be packaged in 50- and 100-pound bags. Soon, the plant was working around the clock.

Men had to be in shape and in good health to work in the mixing department in those days. They lifted 100-pound bags onto a cart, ran the cart to the mixer, opened and hoisted the bags into the mixer, then returned for 50-pound cubes of lard, which were stored in 500-pound barrels.

Sometimes a small overlooked detail could throw the schedule off and shut operations down until the source of the problem was discovered. Once in the mid-1950s, the cake mix refused to rise when it was tested in the new test kitchen. For two weeks tests and more tests were run on tons of cake mix, but no one could discover the problem. Finally chemist Wilbur Hansen realized that the baker had purchased new measuring cups that were inaccurate. "After all that time, we learned that the problem wasn't in the batches of mix at all," William Cole remembered. The wet ingredients hadn't been properly measured—and that had ruined the cake mix.

W ith business booming, the mill was in constant need of expansion to accommodate new equipment, more supplies, and more employees. "The 1950s were good times at the mill," Harry Kealy said. JIFFY's sales were jumping off the charts. To increase the company's storage capacity, the Holmes family decided to add more tanks—and to maximize space, instead of the traditional round shape, they built square tanks. "Big mistake," according to Kealy. "When you put flour in a round tank, you have fifty pounds of pressure all the way around and it balances," he said. "We learned the hard way that in a square tank you've got corners that don't give. They put the square tanks in, and then had to put channel iron around the tanks in the middle to keep them from bulging. One time the seams busted with a full tank of flour. It was about noon on a Saturday, and we thought we heard a tornado rumbling. Then it started to get dusty. Real dusty. The flour covered the basement floor and kept rising. It took us about two weeks to clean that basement up."

Plant additions continued, one after another. In 1955, a warehouse was added to the back of the plant; the following year it was expanded. In 1958 a new administration building was built, and the plant expanded into what had been the old administrative offices. In 1963, the current massive wheat-storage silos rose in Chelsea. Then, with the increased wheat-storage capacity, the flour mill required upgrading. The new windowless building was constructed of slip-formed concrete. The ultramodern pneumatic mill had a wheat storage capacity of 1 million bushels. On December 15, 1964, the *Chelsea Standard* ran an article announcing the addition of the new 3,000-square-foot wheat flour mill:

> *The new building will be equipped as a pneumatic mill—all stocks will be handled, processed and conveyed by air in enclosed bins and conveyors. It will be impossible for foreign matter of any kind to come in contact with the product during the manufacturing and packaging process—from the time the grain is taken in for milling until it has been converted to flour, mixed with other ingredients and comes out as one of the 14 Jiffy Mixes now manufactured by the company . . .*
>
> *Annual output of Jiffy Mixes will reach a total of 600 million packages when the maximum production goal is reached. Currently 200 million packages of Jiffy Mixes are produced for distribution.*

Plant schedules and operations had to keep pace with sales growth. Production hours lengthened and the mill seemed to be in constant need of expansion. In 1966 Chelsea Milling completed construction of a new 3,000-sq.-ft. wheat-flour mill. The windowless building was constructed of slip-formed concrete. The ultramodern pneumatic mill had a wheat-storage capacity of 1 million bushels.

"This was a huge project," Harry Kealy remembered. "We were building a mill when the great majority of mills here in Michigan and throughout the Midwest were closing down." Howard couldn't find skilled engineers and workers to design, build, and equip his new mill, so he had to send to England for help.

With an ever-increasing demand for JIFFY products, and the resulting increase in flour production, Chelsea Milling needed further expansion for the storage of raw materials and finished product. Howard added a third warehouse in 1968 and a fourth two years later.

With the United States market well in hand, Chelsea Milling ventured overseas. In 1961, Howard decided to test market JIFFY in Europe and chose the United Kingdom as the testing ground. "We absolutely overpowered Betty Crocker there," Glenn Lehr remembered. "They couldn't stand our pressure. They folded within six or eight months because JIFFY was by far a better value and better quality."

England, however, was unfamiliar with prepackaged mixes, recalled Lehr. "I don't know how many cakes I baked in the UK to sell the idea to buyers who'd never seen, heard, or thought of a package mix—but it was a lot! We were there two or three years, but England wasn't ready for us. Howard had done a magnificent job of getting the product there, though."

"Howard learned that when you try to sell products in another country, there are all sorts of considerations," Tiny Holmes recalled. "For instance, frosting in England is not the soft, fluffy frostings that Americans are used to. In England, frostings are hard and they crack. Understanding cultural differences is critical when you're introducing a new product."

Sometimes a cultural difference wasn't the only problem, Tiny explained. Howard had hired one English salesman for JIFFY products who wasn't performing up to standards. To discover why, Howard asked to meet him for lunch. The salesman took Howard to his club, perhaps to impress him, but when Howard saw the boards listing club members' golf handicaps, he noticed that his salesman had a handicap of minus one. "Howard knew that no one with that kind of handicap could be working very hard—if at all," Tiny said. "Howard fired the man on the spot, even before eating lunch."

Twins in Appearance Only
The Working Styles of Howard and Dudley

DUDLEY (LEFT) AND HOWARD AT THE INTRODUCTION OF JIFFY CAKE MIXES IN 1958.

Without a doubt, the credit for the mill's longevity and success throughout the twentieth century goes to the two brothers who were identical in looks, but very different in temperament. They often did not see eye to eye, but they worked hard shoulder to shoulder and made decisions with the best interests of the mill, its employees, and consumers in mind.

"Howard and Dudley were identical twins, mirror images of each other, but if you looked at them closely, you could tell the difference," said Lynwood Noah, a friend of both. "Dudley was a smidgen taller, and he was born a half hour earlier than Howard," recalled Noah. "Certainly their personalities were different. Howard worked harder than Dudley. Dudley may have enjoyed life more. But they both had a terrific sense of humor. Together, they were a continuous stitch, a laugh a minute."

William Cole clearly remembers the day he first met the twins at work. He was packing flour at the old mill when a nice-looking man in a brown suit walked up to him, asked how he was doing, talked a bit, then moved on. Fifteen minutes later, the same man—William thought—came by in a blue suit, asked how he was doing, and talked for a while. "That blew my mind!" he recalled with a grin.

Bob Rutherford had a similar experience his first day as a salesman for Chelsea Milling in 1964. When he reported to the mill, he was told that Howard was in Chicago. After introducing himself to June Robinson (whom many people knew as "Peaches"), Rutherford left her office and passed Howard—or a man he thought was Howard—going up the stairs. "He walks by me, doesn't even speak to me," said Rutherford. "So I turn around, march back into Peaches's office, and say, 'I thought you told me Howard was in Chicago. He just came up the stairs!' She starts laughing and tells me that it was his identical twin brother that I'd seen."

Employees at the mill weren't the only ones who could mistake one man for the other. Richard Krafft was a close friend of both brothers— "but no matter how long I knew them, I still had a tough time telling them apart," he admitted. "They both dressed impeccably, in dark blue suits, white shirts, and the same conservative ties. As I say, I knew them very well, but until they started talking, I was never quite sure which was which!"

The company was their life and their livelihood, and they were very good at what they did, said William Cole. "The way they divided responsibilities worked. They worked very hard." He could usually tell the brothers apart by sight (although he had a harder time at night), but he could always identify the brothers by their voices. "Dudley was more hot-tempered and used everyday language. If you made a mistake, he would tell you what he thought, ream you out, then that was that," recalled Cole. "If Howard verbally disciplined you, it would take you fifteen minutes before you realized it."

Howard carried a slide rule wherever he went, and every financial decision he made was based on his calculations on that tool. He could figure the price of wheat, the price of product, and anything else on that slide rule, his office staff remembered.

"Howard was the type of person whose desk was absolutely littered, but he knew where every slip of paper was," said June Robinson. "He wrote on napkins and the backs of envelopes or anything else, as thoughts occurred to him. Every time he went into the mill, he would carry a legal pad because someone would always approach him about something and then he would have a record of it."

But Howard could be as demanding as his brother, Robinson added. "He could never delegate responsibilities.

DUDLEY HOLMES.

I remember once when the parking lot was being paved, Howard was out there drawing the lines, showing the men where to paint. Things had to be done his way."

Sandy Schultz, who took over Robinson's job as Howard's secretary, quickly learned that Howard answered every piece of correspondence he received, even if it was only to say thank you to people who had written saying they liked a product. That attention to detail was evident in everything he did at the mill. "He had tight control over everything that happened here, from the accounts receivable to a worker's bereavement or

HOWARD HOLMES.

a vacation day someone hoped to have," said Schultz. "I quickly saw that he was not a man who liked to be pushed. Howard stuck to his guns."

"My husband was a very hard-working man," Tiny Holmes agreed. "I think he deserved the success he had. He was blessed with great health. Other than a case of appendicitis in college, he was never home sick a day in his life. In fact, he just didn't understand sickness," recalled Tiny. "He worked hard and he expected people to do their share of work. He was very levelheaded. He had no phobias, no drinking problems, nothing that hindered his dedication to his life's work. He was handsome and people liked him. I loved him." The key to Howard's success with people and with the business was based on the fact that he was "a very bright man, very intelligent," said Tiny. "He could read characters pretty well, and he could play their game. He was a likable person selling something people wanted. Anything that made life easier in the kitchen was good for families."

Donald M. Mennel met Howard through the National Soft Wheat Millers' Association. "Howard was always trying to convince us that soft wheat raised in Michigan was superior to all others. He and I

HOWARD HOLMES IN 1970.

used to get into some vigorous discussions," Mennel recalled. Howard was a "political animal," according to Mennel. "He and I both tried to influence legislation a number of times," Mennel explained. They often appeared in Washington together to lobby on behalf of the soft-wheat farmers (who are east of the Mississippi River) to get the same benefits given to the hard-wheat farmers (who are west of the Mississippi). "Our organization improved the growing of wheat and the understanding of wheat," Mennel said. "Almost single-handedly, Howard initiated the Wheat Improvement Program at Michigan State University."

Richard Krafft, chairman of the board and president emeritus of Star of the West Milling Company, worked closely with Howard in championing the MSU program that researched and promoted methods of growing better wheat in a more efficient way. "Howard was the driving force for the program," recalled Krafft. "He launched the wheat research program and then took charge of raising the money to help support the program. It seems that Howard was always in the midst of some fund-raising project to benefit someone somewhere. He had the personality for that. He wasn't a backslapper or overly outspoken, but he had the nice, warm, friendly personality that was hard to say no to. He did great good—more than anyone will ever know."

In the early 1960s, when the Ann Arbor Chamber of Commerce was launching a countywide survey to investigate the possibility of establishing what was to become Washtenaw Community College, committee members repeatedly found doors closed to them—until they took the matter to Howard Holmes. "Within twenty-four hours, Howard had found us the ten-thousand dollars we needed," former WCC trustee Richard Weinrich remembered. "Then without waiting for any thanks, he stepped back and moved on to something else. That's the kind of man he was."

Don Mennel loves to tell a story about Howard's work habits. Once, when Howard and Tiny were flying with the Mennels to San Antonio for a Millers' National Federation convention, the plane stopped for a short time in Dallas. "Being the workaholic that he was, Howard got off the plane to use the phone. We could see him through the window of the plane, talking away," recalled Mennel. "They announced the departure of our plane. He was still talking. They kept announcing final call. He was still talking. They closed the doors and pulled the ramp away. He was still talking. As the plane took off, Tiny waved at him through the plane window and he waved back. He was still talking. Needless to say, Tiny wasn't exactly happy." Mennel finished the story by noting that Howard found another way to get to San Antonio, and arrived before Tiny.

"I've worked in several different places, but Howard Holmes was the best manager I ever worked for," mill employee N. H. Miles said. "He was fair and honest, and if he told you something, you could take it to the bank. His word was his bond. He was an expert on public relations, and that was the key to his success. He thought of his

employees' welfare and feelings as much as he thought of his own."

"Howard was always there for everybody. He was always friendly. He'd never yell at you. If he disciplined you, he'd do it in a calm manner," Cal Summers said, then added that Howard came close to firing him once. "That was when Bill Holmes, Howard's youngest son, came here to work. He was in the warehouse. Howard told me to start Bill at three dollars an hour [this was less than others were paid]. I said, 'Howard, that's not fair.' He told me, 'If you don't think I do things fair, then maybe you don't really belong here.' I said that he wasn't being fair to Billy because he was doing the same work as everyone else. Howard thought about it a minute, then said, 'I guess you're right.'"

Harry Kealy remembers Howard's son Howdy once asking him if he ever knew anyone more stubborn than his father. "I told him, 'Only one—me,'" Kealy recalled with a grin.

"Howard was like a member of your family, but he did expect certain things," said employee Mike Sweet. "He could be a tough person to work for. He ran the whole show—and I mean the *whole* show. No one could turn a screw without asking Howard first."

Howard's secretaries always remembered his personal side. "When I think of Howard, I also think of his sense of humor," recalled Sandy Schultz. "He was always cracking jokes, and he loved nicknames. Mine was 'Sand Man.' He'd call the ladies 'Monsters' and he always referred to his wife, Tiny, as 'The Chief.' He often took her roses, especially on her birthday."

Everyone who knew Howard and Dudley remembered their love for animals. Howard had a menagerie outside his office window. There were statues of rabbits, feeders for squirrels, several bird feeders, and a birdbath with a fountain for winged visitors. A band of cats would roam the mill, catching their own dinners, and Howard's dog, Duffy, supervised operations.

If a bee or a fly (which Howard always referred to as "critters" or "creatures") appeared in the office, it would be scooped up into a paper cup, taken outdoors, and released. After a rain, if Howard saw a worm on the sidewalk, he'd move it onto the grass where it belonged. "He never killed a thing in his life, and he absolutely loved every living creature," Schultz said. Howard had a row of little dog statues

HOWARD WITH HIS FRIEND ZIPPER.

on his desk and pictures of his favorite childhood pony and dog, she remembered. "Every night before he went home, he'd touch his finger to their heads and say, 'Goodnight, Buddy,' 'Goodnight, Buster,' and on down the line. It was a ritual with him."

Donna Lane, who is married to local veterinarian Wilfred Lane, also remembered Howard's love of animals. Once, as the Lane family was about to depart on a vacation, Howard called Dr. Lane to report that an opossum had been hit along the road in Chelsea. They postponed their trip in order for Dr. Lane to tend to the wounded animal. Howard later sent a handsome check, Donna recalled.

Veryl Hafley said that he never saw Howard without a smile on his face. "Howard was one in a million," agreed employee Anna Louise Knickerbocker. "I never looked at him like a boss. He was a friend you could talk to about anything. He came to see us practically every day until a month or two before he died," said Knickerbocker. "He always asked about my family. He came to my wedding. He called and congratulated me in the hospital when my babies were born. He incorporated us into his family, too. I felt that I was part of the Holmes family. Howard was also someone who gave back to the community. He was a man for all seasons."

"Respect is something that you have to earn, and Howard Holmes earned it," said another employee, Luke Collinsworth. "He was very respected, very well-liked. Howard would walk through the plant and would always stop and say something to everyone. He was firm, but he could always make you feel good."

"The brokers and salespeople knew Howard was honest and straightforward, which is rare in the food business," recalled Bob Rutherford. "He worked practically twenty-four hours a day. He generated great warmth and personality. He thought very highly of everyone and he treated everyone alike. Howard was always so professional, in his dress, his mannerisms, his speech." Howard had a habit of laying his gold pocket watch on the table in front of him, to make sure meetings ran quickly and efficiently. "I've had people ask me what happened to that gold watch," said Rutherford.

Rutherford's son, John, had no higher words of praise for Howard than what he told a new employee: "Howard was the kind of man that other men would willingly take a bullet for."

DUDLEY (LEFT) AND HOWARD WORKED TOGETHER FOR NEARLY FIFTY YEARS.

Dudley, the other side of Howard's coin, was the other main reason the mill prospered throughout the years. Their styles worked together in spite of their opposite approaches. "It was fascinating to see how two people who looked so much alike could have such different personalities," recalled Sandy Schultz.

Dudley Jr. remembers his Uncle Howard as "a very easygoing person in dealing with employees—someone who could bawl you out, but you wouldn't figure it out for an hour or two." His father, Dudley Sr., on the other hand, was "instant anger, then the issue was dropped." According to his son, after Dudley Sr. returned from the war "Howard and Dudley pretty much stayed out of each other's way and did their own jobs. They held different points of view, but they were both rowing the boat in the same direction."

"It wasn't just Howard who made this place go. It was also Dudley," Harry Kealy pointed out. "The twins were as different as daylight and dark. I hold both of them up. Dudley was hot-tempered and Howard was bullheaded, but I'd go back to work for them again in a minute."

For forty years, mixing department supervisor William Cole considered Howard and Dudley like brothers—"or maybe fathers"—to him, he said. "They were good, good people. I'd do anything in the world for them, and they'd do the same for me. They trusted me and I trusted them."

When Howard was on the road selling JIFFY products, Dudley Sr. stayed close to the mill and was always available to respond to problems or questions. "Many is the time my phone would ring at two or three a.m., with a crisis," said Dudley Sr. His daughter Diane remembered one late-night call during a snowstorm in the days before citizens-band radios or portable telephones. The sugar trucks hadn't arrived, and production couldn't run without sugar. "Dad climbed into his car to go out looking for the trucks lost in the snow."

Dudley's temper was legendary throughout the plant because it almost always morphed from explosive to humorous. "I have a funny story about Dudley Sr.," Wayne Ruggles said. "Once he ordered too much sugar, and it stayed in a boxcar on the tracks. If it wasn't unloaded within a certain time, we would have had to pay a fine. I was working one Saturday and Dudley asked me, 'Are you gonna get the car unloaded today?' I told him, 'It depends—I'll have to see how much I can get in.' Dudley got mad, walked away, and kicked a tarp. He didn't know that one of our machines was under it. I'll never forget the look on his face when his foot made contact with something unexpected. He came back to me later, as calm as could be, and told me it was all right if I didn't get that sugar unloaded.

"If I was going to get into an argument with one of them, I'd pick Dudley, because Dudley made mistakes and Howard never did," said Ruggles. "You didn't win an argument with Howard. Howard would always ask you to prove everything. Dudley would rave and holler and scream. Then, if you asked him if he was all done, he'd just say, 'Yeah,' and you could reason with him." Mike Sweet agreed with Ruggles. "If you screwed up," said Sweet, "Howard might let you know something about how he felt and then you'd have to think about it. Dudley would yell, get it off his chest, then two minutes later tell you a joke."

"I've had my ups and downs here, but I don't think I could have worked for anybody better than Howard and Dudley," Harry Kealy said. "One was stubborn and bullheaded and if the other gave you hell, you knew it. But they were good men. They also created a helluva good place to work."

JIFFY

LAUGHTER AND TEARS

Recalling Light Moments and Serious Events at the Plant

EMPLOYEES HAVE HAD FUN TOGETHER THROUGH THE YEARS. TOM HALSEY MET UP
WITH A CLOWN AT A COMPANY PICNIC.

Chelsea Milling has always been a family place. Often husbands and wives worked at the mill, leading to some interesting situations. The first day Sue Collinsworth started her job at the plant, one of her fellow workers walked up and told her that the supervisor was "a real good man, a religious man who would never swear or fool around." Collinsworth told her, "I'm glad to hear that—he's my husband!"

And the Holmes family is not the only one to have had successive

HOWARD HAVING FUN IN NORTHERN MICHIGAN, NEAR PETOSKEY.

generations of family members working at the mill. Just a few examples of family succession include Roy Ives, whose father, Wirt Ives, worked there many years; John Rutherford, who followed his father's footsteps into the sales department; and Ron Borders, who followed his mother, Ann, and uncle, Luke Collinsworth, into packaging. After decades working at the mill, June Robinson found retirement easier knowing that her son, Brian, was still a Chelsea Milling employee. These connections often helped facilitate job training and eased retirement transitions, but sometimes there were less desirable results.

One incident many longtime employees remember is the time a man arrived in the plant with a gun. He'd found out that his wife was having an affair with someone who worked there. "I wasn't there that night," recalled Luke Collinsworth, "but I think someone talked him out of doing anything and then called the police."

Another time, when Wayne Ruggles was temporarily put in charge of scheduling the plant crew, someone came to him to complain that his schedule just wasn't going to work. "You've put two women who've been married to the same man on the same line," this person told Ruggles. "There have been a lot of divorces and remarriages within the plant," recalled Ruggles.

"This was a friendly place, and everyone was willing to help each other on the job," Collinsworth said. "Sometimes this was a *very* friendly place—a little Peyton Place. Something seemed to be going on all the time."

Chelsea is still a small town, even today, and since everyone tends to know everyone else, there are very few secrets. Over the years, even townspeople who didn't work at the mill have taken a strong interest in its goings-on, because the company plays such an important role in the local economy.

Occasionally management philosophies have clashed. Harry Kealy remembered one argument he had with Veryl Hafley. "We always got along, but we fought like cats and dogs," said Kealy. (He supervised shipping; Hafley was in packaging.) "Once, I was so mad at him I shut the whole plant down," Kealy recalled. "I was getting boxes with flaps open and I wanted him to glue the boxes. He thought that he had, and he wasn't going to be told otherwise." So Kealy pulled all the switches in the plant. Hafley documented the problem and went to Howard, who went to Kealy for an explanation. The issue was resolved and the switches went back on. Two days later, Dudley heard about the shutdown and asked Kealy about it. "When I told him, Dudley told me, 'the next time, *I'll* help you *myself*,'" Kealy said. "Veryl and I didn't have any grudges after that."

Unfortunately, not all incidents were minor. Serious accidents did occur from time to time, and because employees were so close, everyone at the plant was affected when they happened.

Fire was especially dreaded. In earlier years, the threat of it was constantly present. When a fire alarm sounded, people stopped everything, hearts started pounding, and the mill and town waited anxiously to hear the news. In an atmosphere of highly combustible wheat dust, the threat of fire always looms. The mill suffered at least two devastating fires in the late nineteenth century and another massive one in the early twentieth century. Memories of fires last a long time for employees who were present during one.

HARRY KEALY RAN THE SHIPPING, LOADING, AND RECEIVING FUNCTIONS FOR CHELSEA MILLING. DURING HIS FORTY YEARS WITH THE COMPANY, KEALY SAW MANY IMPROVEMENTS IN THE SAFETY AND RELIABILITY OF OPERATING SYSTEMS.

With the introduction of sprinkler systems and safety regulations, fire became not nearly the threat it had been years ago. But fires can still happen. For example, Veryl Hafley insisted that all his staff wear rubber-soled shoes because he was afraid that footwear with nails might set off a spark. "Still, we used to take awful chances, welding and doing stuff like that," he noted. Once, a fire broke out in the machine shop. Fortunately, it was after sprinklers had been installed—"Otherwise, it could have been disastrous," said Hafley.

On October 17, 1981, an electrically sparked fire damaged part of the mill, and people watched in horror as Dale Horning crawled out through the elevator to the dock yelling, "Don't touch me! Don't touch me!" He had been electrocuted and was afraid of injuring someone else. "That moment still gives me nightmares," Sue Collinsworth recalled.

Dale Horning remembers that day. "It was a Saturday morning, one of those days you really don't want to go to work. I had corn to pick, but I came to work. We used an electric light cord to measure the sugar to see how far down it was in the tank, and that's what I was doing that

"SATURDAY EXPLOSION ROCKS CHELSEA MILLING CO. PLANT," REPORTED THE *CHELSEA STANDARD* ON OCTOBER 13, 1981.

day." The cord had tape every five feet along its length, as a marker. On this particular day the globe fell off the end of the cord, and the electrical wires arced and hit the sides of the metal tank. That caused the dust to explode, knocking Horning down. He was holding onto the cord when the sprinkler system started spraying water, and he was electrocuted. "As soon as the siren went off in the shop, the men shut off the power and that freed me," he said. "The fire shot right out of the tank like a jet. All the metal blew off the wall behind me. I hit the beam, but I don't remember that."

The plant was closed for a week. Horning was in the hospital for seven weeks, with burns over 72 percent of his body. The doctors thought he would lose his hands, but they saved them—"they're all grafted skin," he said. It was a year before he returned to work, and then only part-time. Only once did Horning go back up to the sugar tank. "I didn't want to see it again after that."

Not only did Horning's accident affect everyone within the plant, it also had national consequences. In those days the plant was running around the clock seven days a week, and the warehouse stocked relatively few cases of product. The fire crippled the plant. The lights were off, and production was shut down. Orders had to be filled from the existing stock. "Sales hit a crisis situation," Mike Sweet recalled. "One customer from Woodbridge, New Jersey, was so desperate that he sent his own truck on Saturday to get it loaded, but we had no lights. We got behind two-hundred or three-hundred loads," said Sweet. "When we got back on our feet, at most, we could ship only ten or fifteen loads a day, so we'd have to pick and choose among our customers. Howard didn't want anyone to know that we had no stock. It was a terrible time for Dale and a terrible time for the rest of us. It took months for us to catch up."

Machinery causes trouble when it malfunctions, but even when it's functioning, it is still a constant source of concern. "Lose your concentration for one minute or get careless, and you could be in trouble," said Luke Collinsworth. Shortly after Luke and Sue were married, he got his arm stuck working under a conveyor belt and had to be cut out, resulting in multiple fractures of both bones in one of his arms. The arm was in a cast for a year. Another time, he caught his hand in an auger and had to be rushed to St. Joseph Mercy Hospital; they sewed the hand back in place and secured it with pins.

Sue Collinsworth nearly destroyed the bones of one of her fingers. Cal Clark lost two fingers. "When you work with moving machinery, you have to be very, very careful," said Luke Collinsworth, "and if you don't stop the machine in time, you can get into trouble." Night mechanic Eleanor Isley Klink caught her hand in the box-maker one night. She frantically called around town until she located Veryl Hafley in a Chelsea restaurant. He rushed to the plant, grabbed Eleanor, and took her to the doctor. "Many nights I got calls, sometimes as many as three times a night, with some problems," Hafley remembered. "I always dreaded hearing that the problems were medical emergencies."

In 2000, a year after Luke Collinsworth retired, a man-lift malfunctioned, dropping his nephew Ron Borders from the third floor of an elevator shaft into the pit at the bottom. Borders lay there crumpled until the fire department arrived, rushed him into an ambulance, and delivered him to the hospital. The accident left him permanently paralyzed from the waist down.

Fortunately, it isn't just serious accidents that have brought mill employees together. Holiday lunches, going-away and retirement parties, summer barbecues, Christmas parties, football pools, and spur-of-the-moment celebrations are just a few of the ways employees have chosen to party together. And in every department, at every level, there have been pranks and jokes—lots of lighthearted, harmless jokes.

Harry Kealy was the target of endless pranks. Back in 1976 he was asked to make some deliveries one day. Unbeknownst to him, one of the men in trucking had unhooked the trailer before his truck had left the garage. It was a foggy day, and Kealy was concentrating on his driving as he and the truck crept along the highway at twenty miles an hour. "I had gotten as far as the truck stop at Baker Road—about eight miles from the plant—before I realized that I wasn't pulling a trailer," recalled Kealy. "I was some mad."

One Saturday morning while Kealy was working at the plant, Dudley Jr. called and asked him to hurry over to the East Middle Street house. When he got there, Dudley was waiting for him in the garage. "I walked all the way over to that garage. Dudley pushed a button to open the door, got in his car, wound down the window, and asked me to close the garage door for him!" said Kealy. "He could hear what I thought of that joke as he drove down the street."

Throughout the years, employees frequently enjoyed coming together for company gatherings. Top 2 photos, left to right: Wayne Penic, Dick Cole, Billy Scott, and Ted Quigley. Alice Jones and Albert Doll. Right: Howard and Tiny Holmes with Cal Summers.

Mike Sweet was driving to work one April Fools' Day, when he heard on the car radio that the Detroit Zoo received a huge overload of calls on April Fools', more than at any other time of the year. "We were shipping everything by rail in those days, and we frequently had to trace lost shipments," Sweet said. "I wrote the zoo's number on a pink slip and asked Tom Halsey to follow up on a lost shipment by dialing that number. Tom spent all day trying to get through, not realizing until the end that it was a joke."

The Holmes family's children were prime targets for some of the most outrageous jokes. "Pranks and sabotage happen in every workplace in America," Howdy said. "There's always the thought, 'Let's have fun with the new guy or gal.' If the new person is also the son or

TOP: MIKE SWEET, KARYN HORTON, DOUG MONTGOMERY, STEPHEN NOSE, JAN SWEET, AND ARLENE HONBAUM; ABOVE: JUNE ROBINSON, HELEN DORER, MAXINE BRAINARD. RIGHT: LYNN JONES AND RAY ZIEGLER.

daughter of the company president, the stakes rise."

The most common prank is still enjoyed as much today as it was when Howdy was a young employee. "We call it the 'Cocoa Fly Experience,'" said Howdy. Cocoa comes in fifty-pound bags with a tear string. Mixers rip open a bag, hoist it onto their shoulders, and empty the bag into the mixer. They shake the bag to get as much cocoa out as possible, and the residue is a fine, powdery dust. "The trick comes after the empty bags are left on the floor," explained Howdy. "The newcomer is asked if he checked the bag for cocoa flies. He gets down to look, then someone stomps on the bag and the powder covers him. That trick still works, decades after my own cocoa-fly experience."

Part of the family's tradition is to make sure that Holmes children get experience in every department. "I loaded boxcars. I worked as a line operator in packaging. I worked in the mixing department. And, wherever I was, there was some form of 'gotcha!'" remembered Howdy. "The warehouse had a huge conveyor system that sorted all our products. From this conveyor we'd take the stock and load it into the boxcar. There's an art to that," he said. "The trick is to load from the outsides of the car to the middle. It was always me who had to throw the crucial cases into the middle correctly—if I missed, the loading would have to be readjusted and that was a lot of work. I'd always miss. Then I'd become responsible for the overtime needed to load the car correctly."

Fifteen years later, Howdy said, he finally realized that when he was heading to that crucial box, someone would accelerate the rate of boxes coming down the conveyor. "Bury him now," someone would whisper. And Howdy would be buried in boxes.

"Bury him now," someone would whisper. And Howdy would be buried in boxes.

"That's fun for everyone," he said. "If someone won't kid with you, then you have to worry. I was often the butt of jokes, but I felt like a part of the gang.

"Harry Kealy was personally behind most of the shenanigans involving me, but I had one heck of a grand finale to the 'gotchas!'" Howdy recalled with a grin. One weekend when no one was around, Howdy, then a teenager, took a high-low forklift and moved countless double stacks of finished inventory. Then he drove the machine into the middle of the stacks and moved all the pallets back into place, hiding the forklift completely. "It took Harry Kealy two days to find that high-low," Howdy recalled with satisfaction. "It was like winning the Olympics." Kealy finally discovered the forklift when he climbed up onto something high, looked around the warehouse, and saw the gap between the boxes.

"My father warned me that I'd have to be three times as good as anybody else," Howdy remembered. " 'Everyone's going to watch you closely,'" he warned. "He was right.

"My father's personal belief was 'What's good for one is good for all' and 'if anything, be more difficult on a Holmes,'" recalled Howdy. "He was trying to build character in his offspring. He was absolutely right—though I would not have conceded that at the time."

THE FOURTH GENERATION

Preparing for a Gradual Handoff

HOWARD SUMNER HOLMES AND HOWARD SAMUEL HOLMES (HOWDY) WORKED TOGETHER FOR
SEVERAL YEARS AFTER HOWDY RETURNED TO CHELSEA MILLING IN 1987.

By the time Howard's new secretary, Sandy Schultz, met the boss's older son in 1987, Howdy was a renowned race-car driver and author. "Probably to many people, Howdy's coming into the family business was a surprise, but it was something Howdy felt he had to do," said Schultz. "He worked his way into the business gradually, watching what his father did, and in time, taking on more responsibilities."

When Howdy returned to the mill, he joined his brother Bill and cousin Dudley as the fourth generation of the family in management. Dudley Holmes Jr., who had joined the family business in 1969, was in the process of taking over his father's purchasing responsibilities, and, eventually, the title of vice president of purchasing; he was also responsible for plant safety and maintenance. Bill had moved into the office next to his father's and was supervising environmental issues, recycling, and government compliance; he was also splitting his time between Chelsea Milling and the National Guard while taking fighter-pilot training.

Like their father and uncle before them, Bill and Howdy didn't always see eye to eye on how to run the company. "Bill was less interested in changing the routine here; he was more interested in enhancing what we were doing," Howdy said. "My brother and I were equally principled in our approaches; we just had different viewpoints. He was 'Steady as you go' and I was 'Let's change everything here.' Neither was right or wrong, just different."

"To generations of people in the food industry, Howard Holmes was Chelsea Milling."

Where race car driving had always been Howdy's passion, flying had become Bill's. When he got the chance to become a commercial pilot, Bill took it, and left the day to day running of the mill to his brother. He continues to serve on the company's board of directors.

Any transition between leaders tends to be difficult. The transition between Howard and Howdy as leaders of the company was no exception. It was hard for everyone, remembered Mike Sweet. "We all knew that Howard was slipping while still trying to run a multimillion-dollar company," said Sweet. "We all knew that a lot of things needed changing. But a lot of us had been there a long time, and change can come hard."

"To generations of people in the food industry, Howard Holmes *was* Chelsea Milling," said Bob Rutherford. "This was Howard's baby, his life."

The first sign to all employees that change was in the air came on a November day shortly after Howdy arrived. The plant was falling far

Two generations of leadership—Howard and Howdy Holmes.

TINY AND HOWARD HOLMES.

behind in filling orders, although it was running thirteen lines around the clock and storing product in temporary warehouses in Jackson. "That wasn't enough," said Mike Sweet. In the midst of all this, Safeway stores called and asked for a rush order of four truckloads of product. "We had to make a decision about who would get product and who wouldn't," recalled Sweet. "This was something that Howard often had to do, but it was Howdy's first experience with the situation." Howdy reluctantly called Sweet, telling him that the Safeway request needed to be filled and that someone else's order was going to be bumped. "That's never going to happen again," Howdy told Sweet, and it never did.

Howdy added four new packaging lines, doubled the warehouse space, streamlined warehouse procedures, and hired employees with experience in finance, food sales, marketing, and production to share administrative duties with him. He upgraded equipment so that the mixing process became more efficient, and computerized the test kitchens, so less baking was required but more exact calibrating could be done. He also called frequent staff and administrative meetings. "Howdy asked us to give presentations about our jobs, to think and plan along the team concept," said Sweet.

"Howdy's team approach to management lets others invest their talents and ideas into the company," explained Howdy's wife, Carole. "This style is the product of wanting a strong family life. He's surrounded by bright, intelligent people who are dedicated to the Chelsea Milling Company," said Carole, "so he can step back and attend a hockey game with our son and not worry about what is happening at the mill every minute. Howard's era was different."

"Howdy's skills are appropriate for the times because all businesses these days are run very differently," said his mother, Tiny. "The computer has changed everything. The ways my husband and my son approach business are entirely different. Their principles are the same, but the ways they apply them are very different. However, Chelsea Milling still makes reasonably priced, high-quality products for the public. The company's focus is still not on how much money we can make, but how to make people happy and answer their needs."

Carole Holmes said that her husband "never struggled to fill Howard's shoes. He knew that he had shoes of his own to walk in and that he'd been taught well."

In 1997, the *Wall Street Journal* noted that while Howdy Holmes stuck by his father's longtime commitment to avoid advertising, he did alter Chelsea Milling's age-old box design. The article went on to point out:

> He insists that without the changes "Jiffyville," as he calls it, would be in serious decline. Outside directors agree. "It wasn't going to stay profitable," says Wilbur K. Pierpont, a director and former financial vice president at the University of Michigan [now deceased]. "It was floundering," adds Everett Everson, the other outside director and a retired professor of crop science at Michigan State University. "We were of the opinion they might have to sell the company." Both men are old friends of the Holmes family.

Howdy Holmes made some decisions rapidly, while other changes came gradually. He believed—and continues to believe—that drastic measures were necessary at that time. "My intent," he told the *Wall*

Street Journal reporter, "is to move a hundred-year-old business from a proprietorship to the early stages of professional management."

According to Wayne Ruggles, during the transition between father and son, the company changed from a family-style to a corporate-style workplace. "Everyone had reported directly to Howard, but Howdy is establishing several layers of reporting up the ladder," said Ruggles. "Howdy also understands and has a vision for what is needed in machinery."

At one point, Howdy even brought in a psychologist to advise the family about the dynamics of change. Several years after Howdy moved into the company's management, Jess Meininger wrote, "Howdy is doing a job that should have been done several years ago. I get a quarterly report and the things that he's doing in that mill are great! The overall operation, quality control, and intelligent people he has hired are all bringing the mill into a new age. There were things done when I was there that I thought should be changed, but you couldn't get Howard to change anything. Still, I have nothing but admiration for Howard and Dudley."

After fifty years of running the business pretty much the same way, jobs were suddenly being redefined and realigned. In January 1984, Dudley Sr. announced his retirement, and two weeks later he was gone, without training anyone to fill his place. Bob Rutherford retired in 1990, leaving the position of director of sales open. New faces began appearing on the management team; they came from all over the country.

Howdy told the *Milling Journal* during a 1998 interview:

> *The biggest change was teaching our people to think in a different way. . . . Communications need to go in every direction, not just up and down the corporate ladder. I see the company president and the guy in sanitation as equal — they both have something to say about how things are run.*

That same year, *Michigan History* magazine reported:

> *Howdy's attitude toward his employees is unique. He calls them Team Jiffy and treats them as an extended family. The company's mission statement summarizes the spirit: "The mission of Team Jiffy is to achieve 100 percent product integrity with quality people caring about each other." A longevity bulletin board in the plant lists employees who have been with the company for twenty to forty years.*
>
> *At a time when many corporations are downsizing, the CMC considers its 350 employees when making corporate decisions. Howdy firmly believes that "people — not equipment — are the most important asset. After all, they are the heart of the company."*

Although some faces at the company were new, Howdy was determined to maintain the basic people-based principles established by the generations of family businessmen before him. Howdy asserted to John U. Bacon for an article in the *Detroit News* business section in 1998:

> *Some of the old ways we're talking about aren't the old ways of doing things but the old ways of thinking about things, Holmes says. Things like principles, integrity, honesty, loyalty. Those aren't going to change.*

While personnel changes were happening, the plant was receiving a major face-lift, becoming significantly safer and cleaner. In Howdy's first ten years, the company boosted milling capacity from 2,500 to 4,500 hundredweights per day and had an increase in ready-mix production of 23 percent. A new 125,000-square-foot warehouse was constructed for finished products. Modern statistical control processes were added, and near-infrared analysis equipment was installed in the quality assurance laboratory.

Mike Sweet credits Dudley Jr. with improvements made in plant cleanliness and safety. So does employee Phyllis Stepp, who said, "Employees want to produce something they can be proud of and work in a clean, pleasant place. The plant is a lot cleaner than it has ever been. With new technology, keeping things up in the plant is much easier. There is a lot of pride here."

As this all started happening, people were watching Howard's reactions carefully. "It was difficult for Howard to ease off working here," recalled Mike Sweet. In fact, as late as 1997, Howard had joked to Gabriella Stern of the *Wall Street Journal* that "In another 500 years, I'll be ready to retire," adding, "I've enjoyed every day I've been here."

Employees began to notice that Howard's memory was slipping. At first he seemed tired or forgetful, but when the situation didn't improve, people looked again. "It was easy enough to see that something was wrong because Howard had always had a very sharp memory," Wayne Ruggles recalled. "I suggested to Howdy that he get Howard checked. We noticed that he could remember who sharpened what pencil in kindergarten, but he couldn't remember what we had talked about that day."

Sandy Schultz remembers the exact day when she realized that Howard wasn't himself. "It was a snowy winter day, and he came into the office and said he didn't feel good," she said. "He'd shoveled a huge drift of snow in front of his garage, he told me. Suddenly, he began repeating different things. He never seemed quite the same again."

Howdy quietly began to provide supervision behind the scenes. Schultz found a number of handwritten notes from Howdy to Howard saying things like, "Dad, while trying to find something for Sandy in your office Friday, I saw several personal bills which were unpaid and late—want some help with them? H2." Above the note, Howard had

ON THE TWINS' 82ND BIRTHDAY IN 1995, HOWARD WAS PRESENTED WITH A FLAGPOLE, AND HE RAISED THE FIRST FLAG HIMSELF. DUDLEY IS BEHIND HIM, AND SANDY SCHULTZ IS TO HIS LEFT.

drawn a sad face and a comment: "*Merci*—nope!"

Eventually the suspicion of Alzheimer's was confirmed. The Holmes family began working with the Chelsea Methodist Home to fund a facility devoted to Alzheimer's patients. Schultz continued to work closely with Howard, but also spent increasingly more time with Howdy. "As Howard's illness progressed, he continued to make decisions, but Howdy would oversee everything to make sure they were on the right track," recalled Schultz. "No one wanted to see Howard leave. It was painful to watch the deterioration of a great mind."

HOWARD AND HIS SPECIAL CAREGIVER, ROSEMARY ESCH, VISIT WITH ROSEMARY'S UNCLE, EMPLOYEE LESTER ESCH, DURING A MORNING WALK IN THE PLANT. THIS WAS LATE IN HOWARD'S ILLNESS.

When chief financial officer Douglas Tomney arrived in 1993, he discovered that Howard had a sharp, intuitive mind—"quite brilliant, really." Tomney would have to ask to borrow the executive ledger from Howard to get any work done—and Howard relinquished it reluctantly. "He was a very fine financial person, and I always had to be prepared to answer probing questions adequately," remembered Tomney. "Howard knew the right questions to ask, and he could make you wriggle if you didn't have the right answers."

Within a few years, however, Howard would ask questions and discuss the financials, then ask the same questions over and over again. "Howard was still president and CEO, and Howdy was technically vice president of sales and administration, but we all knew that Howdy was making everything happen," Tomney said. "He had to tread carefully at times, though, working behind the scenes."

With a new awareness of the disease, the family also wanted

to educate company employees. Howdy invited in an expert to talk about the signs and progress of Howard's illness. "Our goal was to maintain his dignity," said Sandy Schultz. "Everyone did their best to help. We all thought the world of Howard." The experts explained that Alzheimer's patients do best if they can remain in familiar surroundings. For over fifty years, the mill had been a seven-days-a-week job for Howard. The Holmes family believed that Chelsea Milling should continue to remain the biggest part of Howard's life for as long as possible.

No one remembers just when Howard relinquished the last managerial ties with the company, the process was so gradual and gentle, but eventually he was only able to make his traditional rounds in the office and plant, to greet people and watch the machinery pour, package, and transport. "Knowing of his illness and what was to come," recalled Howdy, "our family tried to maximize the quality of his life."

During the last few years of his life, Howard spent increasingly more time with his brother—"and they were entertaining together!" said Howdy. "They badgered each other nonstop. It was fun to see two immaculately dressed old-fashioned gentlemen go at it." The extended Chelsea Milling family made every effort to strengthen the late-in-life relationship between Howard and Dudley, who had often been at odds with each other throughout their professional years. Dudley had spent several years away from the plant, but had started walking again to the mill from his East Middle Street house, just as he had every day for five decades. Sandy Schultz made lunch dates for the two brothers so that they could spend more time together.

At first, it seemed that Dudley's memory was failing faster than his brother's. His family had taken the battery out of his black Cadillac so he could no longer drive. "He was a menace behind the steering wheel," said Mike Sweet. But Dudley was always capable of thinking up creative tricks. When his car was no longer working, he just walked to the mill and borrowed Howard's car. "The Chelsea police in town didn't know the difference between the brothers," according to Sweet, "so they didn't know to stop Dudley from driving. In the end, Howdy had to take measures to get Howard off the road, and both brothers finally lost the use of a car."

"Remarkably, neither Howard nor Dudley ever lost their social graces," recalled Schultz. "In their last years, they might not have a clue who you were, but you'd never know it. Their mother taught them well when they were little. This mill had been Howard and Dudley's responsibility all their lives, and they knew they belonged here—even when they no longer understood why."

Everyone at the mill tried to help; many went to great lengths to show their appreciation for Howard's thoughtfulness over the years. Nearly every day, Schultz would drive Howard to and from the milling company for his daily rounds. To make sure he wouldn't miss a day, John Rutherford was assigned to be backup driver. Rutherford, Douglas Tomney, and others would take turns escorting the brothers around the plant, and then take them to Gina's restaurant for a lunch that always ended with a round of hot fudge sundaes. That routine lasted for several years, until Howard was no longer able to conduct conversations. After that, the family hired a caregiver. But Howard's rounds of Chelsea Milling continued, still followed by lunch and ice cream.

More than one new employee hired in the 1990s said that his or her decision about whether or not to accept a job at Chelsea Milling was made after seeing how much Howdy and the company's employees cared for the two elderly brothers. "You have to respect a company that will accommodate people the way this one does," said Jack Kennedy.

HOWARD (LEFT) AND DUDLEY LATE IN LIFE.

Driving Toward the Future
Howdy's Story

Named Indianapolis 500 Rookie of the Year in 1979, Howdy went on to race in six Indy 500s; he achieved the best average finishing record of anyone who started four or more races in the history of that race. Howdy is with Rick Mears and Tom Sneva after qualifying with them for front-row positions at the 1984 Indy 500.

Howard and Dudley Holmes steered the company through a family tragedy, the Depression, World War II, major ups and downs in the economy, and the boom days of the package-mix industry. It was up to the family's fourth generation to steer the company into the twenty-first century, with former race car driver Howdy Holmes at the wheel.

"You have to give my father and uncle a tremendous amount of credit and recognition for their accomplishments," Howdy said. "When my grandfather Howard Samuel Holmes died in 1936, his two sons were thrown into the deep end of the business without any business experience whatsoever. At the age of twenty-three, no one really knows very much about themselves or the world. Unlike my generation, they hadn't even spent much time hanging around the mill. Everything they learned about business they learned through trial and error. They witnessed a tremendous evolution in the business world."

Howdy and his brother Bill were raised at the mill, doing a variety of jobs over the years. "I worked all over the place, at first for gas money to feed my car," recalled Howdy. "Howard [his father] was always very accommodating with his children. There was never any pressure to work at Chelsea Milling." Howard did emphasize several important ideas to his children, however. He told them that it was important to show that they were willing to do anything that was asked of them, and that "it's not what you say that counts, but what you do." He also stressed that if the boys would do everything assigned without arguing or making a long face, the mill's longtime employees would accept them. The secret of Chelsea Milling, Howard told his boys, is that the owners are not any different from anyone else—and Howdy and Bill would have to demonstrate that in their behavior.

As a youngster, Howdy's first job at the mill was to sweep floors. Next, he was tied to a rope, given a broom and lowered inside the silos so that he could clean the silo walls. "It's not the most popular job in the plant—which is why newcomers get it," Howdy noted with a grin. "I painted in places that had no ventilation. I worked in the flour mill and the mixing department and came away at the end of the day covered in flour dust."

As he grew older, Howdy loaded boxcars, helped in the mixing department, worked as a line operator in packaging, and drove the high-low in the warehouse. "I benefited tremendously from working here," Howdy said. "There isn't a job here that I haven't done, so I know what is—and isn't—reasonable to expect. I saw how my father interacted with people, and that seemed pretty fair to me; I try to use his style as a role model."

After high school, Howdy attended Northwood Institute in Midland, Michigan, then Washtenaw Community College and Eastern Michigan University. Between colleges, he was working at the mill in 1968 when an advertisement for a private drivers' school at the Michigan International

Speedway arrived in the mail. That letter gave him the push he needed to act on a boyhood dream, and led to a twenty-year career in racing. During his senior year at EMU, Howdy told his parents that he definitely intended to go into the family business, but first needed to follow his dream. "I just didn't know that it would be *twenty years* of living my dream!" he recalled many years later.

Racing was an interest Howdy shared with all of his family, and they traditionally attended the Indy 500 races together. Every Memorial Day weekend, Howard and Tiny would pack the five children into their car and head to Indianapolis, stopping at Pokagon State Park to dine on crispy chicken and deviled eggs, then checking in at the Elwood Court Motel near Elmore, Indiana, before heading off to the races. "I was twelve or so when the idea formed in my head that racing cars must be a pretty cool thing to do," Howdy said. "I didn't know about the minor leagues of sports car racing; my introduction was to the pinnacle—the Indy 500."

He didn't start racing until he was twenty-three, later than most drivers begin. In 1970, he got his license from the Sports Car Club of America Driving School; afterward, he earned his license from the International Motor Sports Association. Between racing schools, he worked for two years as a "go-fer" for John Stringer, who had a small business called Road Sport International. Howdy purchased a small single-seat Formula Ford, a beginning class, from Road Sport International. The men in the Chelsea Milling warehouse built him an eight-by-twenty-foot plywood garage in the warehouse, and Howdy set to work to learn everything he could about cars. He ordered a set of tools from an *Auto World* catalog for $69.95 (he still has the tools), found an engine manual at Ulrich's bookstore in Ann Arbor, and then bought a Ford Econoline van. A friend helped him build a trailer, and he was in business.

Howdy spent eighteen or nineteen hours a day in that plywood garage, taking the engine of the Formula Ford out and rebuilding it over and over again. During his first year, he raced in twenty-one regional and national events, finishing in nineteen of them. "If I was going to do it, I wanted to be the best," he said. He won the regional championship and came close to winning the national championship. "It was a year of baptism by fire," he remembered. He wrote columns for racing and trade

WHEN HOWDY WAS IN HIS EARLY TWENTIES, RACING BECAME A PASSION FOR HIM. FRIENDS AT CHELSEA MILLING BUILT HIM A GARAGE WHERE HE COULD LEARN THE INTRICACIES OF BUILDING AND REPAIRING MOTORS.

publications, then a book called *Formula Car Technology*. When he started, there was very little information about the racing business; he had to learn everything on his own. "My book was my chance to offer some help and advice," Howdy said, while glancing at the mementos from these days that fill his office at Chelsea Milling.

"Racing was my life. All of my life. Every waking moment was devoted to making it work," he said. "When someone is really passionate about what they do, they're passionate about every aspect of what they do." He won the Sports Car Club of America Central Division championship in 1972 and 1973, and was named Labatt's North American Formula Atlantic Champion in 1978, Canadian Driving Champion in 1978, and Indianapolis 500 Rookie of the Year in 1979. Between 1979 and his retirement from racing in 1988, he competed in six Indy 500s and achieved the best average finishing record in the race's history for those who started in four or more races.

In 2000 Howdy took several people from Chelsea Milling to the Indy

500; while sitting in the crowd of 450,000 people, he realized how very few were fortunate enough to be able to say they had "been there and done that," he said. "It's a pretty small club and I'm proud to be a member.

"I went into racing because I wanted to follow my boyhood dream. Very few people get the opportunity to truly pursue their dreams. It was all about the personal challenge to excel. I learned that there's no bigger competitor than oneself." Howdy paused for a moment and then added, "I had to learn on my own that rewards come from growing, not staying still. Once you reach your destination, if you don't set out on another trip, you're stranded. It's not the destination, but the journey, that's important."

By 1983 Howdy was looking toward his exit from racing. Two years later, at the age of thirty-eight, he began planning his return to Chelsea Milling, hoping to avoid friction with his father, uncle, brother, and cousin. "The race-car-driver syndrome was working against me big-time, but I knew that I was coming with a full deck: the knowledge of advertising, negotiations, structuring business deals, journalism, TV work, sales, marketing, working with companies of all sizes," he said. "I'd learned all this by trial and error throughout my twenty years in the motor sports business."

In November 1987, Howdy returned to Chelsea Milling. His wife, Carole, was pregnant with their son, and he had one more season of racing to complete and a new business to learn. "Those were crazy days," he recalled.

"Why did I return to the family business?" asked Howdy. "My father said it best once to a reporter: 'When you get into the flour business, it sifts into your mind and you become too dumb to get out of the business.' Before I left, I told my dad I would return some day. This business is in my family's blood."

From the start, "I sort of acted like the CEO," Howdy said. "That

"I THINK THE REASON THAT SO MANY [FAMILY BUSINESSES] ARE DOOMED TO FAILURE," SAID HOWDY, "IS BECAUSE IT'S SO DIFFICULT TO SEPARATE THOUGHTS FROM FEELINGS WHEN DEALING WITH FAMILY MEMBERS."

seemed pretty natural to me, though probably pretty unnatural to a lot of other people!" Just as Howard and Dudley had been forced to determine the division of responsibilities in 1936 when their father died, and again after Dudley returned from war, Howdy and Bill had to do the same in 1987. "My return didn't take my father by surprise. I think he appreciated the help from the two of us," said Howdy. "After fifty-one years, however, he had established a routine, and I was about to change the environment."

The fourth generation of the Holmes family at the mill faced more than personal and personnel issues, however. The odds are long against a family business surviving the second generation, let alone the fourth. According to statistics, only one in four family-owned businesses survives to the second generation, and only one in twelve of those will survive to the third generation.

There are no statistics to predict the probability of success for a fourth-generation family business. People who build their own businesses do the jobs of many people, often around the clock—as Howard did. They have a hand in every decision that is made, every item or product that is purchased, every package that comes off the conveyor belt. "They have no time to take a breath, look around, and think about other ways of doing things," said Howdy. "Eventually, sole proprietorships reach a point where they're not exposed to new ideas and the company stops growing and stops keeping pace with the marketplace." That was the situation he found when he returned to Chelsea Milling.

The crucial factor behind the success or failure of most family businesses is the choice of a successor to the founder. "I think the reason that so many are doomed to failure is because it's so very difficult to separate thoughts from feelings when dealing with family members," said Howdy. "Often the situation forces the head of the family to make a choice and that can be excruciatingly painful. They see the choice as sending a message suggesting that one child or relative is more capable or qualified than another—and how can you do that? Business decisions are not made with your heart or family decisions with your head. Business owners have to recognize that their children are different and that, although they appreciate the differences, some characteristics make for a better CEO."

The odds are long against a family business surviving the second generation, let alone the fourth.

Howdy arrived ready to "go toe-to-toe" with his father and help the company move toward a new century. Years later he commented, "I really wanted to help, but my idea of helping meant calling most of the shots. I didn't immediately realize that I needed to recalibrate to my new environment. My pace was a function of my most recent environment; it was very fast." In contrast, the pace at Chelsea Milling was "glacial—to be generous," he said. "When I talked about trying to get the company into the next century, I was talking *twentieth century!*"

When Howdy arrived, the company still had some rotary telephones, few computers, no fax machines, no e-mail, and a Victorian-style daily

HOWDY INTRODUCES HIS SON, HOWDY, TO ANOTHER FORM OF TRANSPORTATION. "I GREW UP IN THE MILL. TOURING THE PACKAGING AREA AND WORKING IN THE WAREHOUSE HAVE BEEN A WAY OF LIFE FOR THE KIDS IN OUR FAMILY," SAID HOWDY.

routine that called for shutting down the switchboard for lunch. On the other hand, Chelsea Milling had some outstanding and impressive assets going for it: a history of leadership with great compassion, a well-defined niche in the food business, and tremendous loyalty from its employees.

The first thing Howdy did was to make a list of everything that he thought needed attention. "After filling both sides of the paper with little and big things, such as education, training, repairs, replacements, concepts, procedures, consistency, and fairness, I stopped. That was

enough to start with. I still have that list," he said. He ran into formidable roadblocks, particularly with the people who had been associated with the company for many years and were resisting any change.

He quickly realized that he had to create new positions to run this very old company effectively in the new, fast-paced, and quickly changing world. But the faster Howdy tried to go, the slower the progress seemed to be. "It finally dawned on me that to be effective, I had to change my ways—and I did," he recalled. "It was all worth it. I wouldn't have done that if I hadn't been passionate about my goals."

About that time, a friend gave Howdy a cartoon he thought was appropriate—and he still keeps it on his desk to remind him of his early years on the job. "That caption— 'I hate stampeding alone!' —perfectly describes how I felt," Howdy recalled. "I came racing in here, ready to make great changes and have people join in behind me. It didn't happen that way. Anything worth doing is worth doing well—and no important things come easily."

In spite of the difficulties in leadership transition, Chelsea Milling was prospering to the point of capturing media attention. National business publications soon developed a fascination with the little company that was a giant in its field. On June 11, 1990, *Forbes* magazine reported:

> Today the Holmes' Chelsea Milling Co. . . . mixes up over 1 million boxes a day of Jiffy brand biscuit, muffin and cake mixes. . . . The Holmeses have a profitable 14% of the biscuit mix business and about 50% of the $100 million muffin mix business, augmented by a very small share in cakes and icings.

Among the Holmes clan's most effective weapons is aggressive pricing. . . . Chelsea can keep its prices so low by spending little money on packaging and no money on advertising, except for promotions with grocery stores.

A December 2001 article in *Fortune* magazine asked:

Just how has Chelsea Milling beat the big boys at their own game for more than 70 years? . . . It helps if you don't play by the same rules. Jiffy doesn't spend a dime on marketing—but can turn on one—and keeps prices low. It also helps that the current president and CEO, Howdy S. Holmes, realized a while back that bringing outsiders into the old family operation was the key to building a modern company.

The *Fortune* article also noted that Howdy scoffs at the suggestion that he's trying to keep up with the world's Betty Crockers and Duncan Hineses. "Strictly speaking, they are trying to keep up with us," he informed the reporter. At the time the *Fortune* article was written, Chelsea Milling Company was leading the pack in the then $230 million-dollar-a-year muffin-mix category, capturing 30.6 percent of the revenue and a whopping 55.3 percent share of unit sales. It's even more impressive when you consider that these figures were achieved by a small family-run operation weathering a leadership transition. It's no wonder that Chelsea Milling was appropriately dubbed the Little Giant in the muffin-mix industry.

But while national media attention was increasing, the market share was ratcheting up, and Howdy was slowly taking over leadership of the company, the most important things remained unchanged. Employee Wayne Ruggles aptly pointed out, "We still make a good product and we keep the price down. I think that Howdy, like his father, has a handle on where the profit is and the relationship between quality and quantity."

On September 22, 1995, eight years after returning to the family business, Howdy signed the papers officially making him CEO of the Chelsea Milling Company. By that time, he had already begun implementing a long list of changes, but his pride in becoming CEO was overshadowed by his concern for his father. "To me, it was a very sad torch-passing," recalled Howdy, "watching my father deteriorate before my eyes."

HOWARD AND DUDLEY
The Twins Leave Their Legacies

HOWARD RECEIVED AN HONORARY DEGREE FROM CLEARY COLLEGE IN 1983 FOR HIS CONTRIBUTIONS TO BUSINESS AND THE COMMUNITY, INCLUDING HIS WORK AS PRESIDENT OF THE CHELSEA MILLING COMPANY, VICE PRESIDENT AND DIRECTOR OF C&S CARTON COMPANY, DIRECTOR OF THE EXECUTIVE COMMITTEE OF THE MILLERS' NATIONAL FOUNDATION, TREASURER OF THE WHEAT INDUSTRY COUNCIL, AND MEMBER OF THE DOMINO'S PIZZA BOARD OF DIRECTORS.

D uring his later years, while his role as leader of Chelsea Milling was winding down, Howard Holmes was showered with awards, plaques, certificates, and letters thanking him for his service to everything from agriculture and milling to the Boy Scouts, Detroit's food kitchens, St. Joseph Mercy Hospital, the town of Chelsea, the state of Michigan, the Ronald McDonald House in Ann Arbor, the University of Michigan, the YMCA, and local churches, whose announcements he paid for in the *Chelsea Standard* every week for decades.

ON MARCH 24, 1988, MICHIGAN STATE UNIVERSITY RECOGNIZED HOWARD FOR HIS LIFETIME
COMMITMENT TO THE MSU WHEAT IMPROVEMENT PROGRAM. STANDING TO HOWARD'S LEFT
ARE CAROLE, HOWDY, AND TINY HOLMES. TO HIS RIGHT ARE MSU'S GORDON GUYER AND
WENDY AND BILL HOLMES.

But in the end, the thanks that mattered the most to Howard came
from the people he had worked with for more than a half century. Those
tributes came more informally in the form of hugs, smiles, concerned
phone calls, endless tours of the plant, rides, lunches at Gina's restaurant,
visits, and a huge collage that decorated his bedroom at the end of his life.

During the twin brothers' declining years, family members finally
had the chance to relax with the duo, as they never had done when
Howard and Dudley were hard at work. "Later in life, Howdy and his
father were the best of friends," Carole Holmes recalled. "They nurtured
each other. I might be talking with Howdy on the phone and he would
pause, then come back on and say, 'Dad just walked in and gave me a
hug.' As Howard got older and more and more frail, he became much
more affectionate."

Sandy Schultz clearly remembers Howard's last day at work, on
October 27, 2000. Shortly afterward, he was admitted to the Chelsea
Methodist Retirement Home's new Towsley Center Alzheimer facility,

built with the assistance of the Holmes family.

Every day Harry Kealy would check in on his former boss at the center, joking about the latest happening at the mill, or the old days, or the good looks of the on-duty nurse. When Howard died on January 3, 2001, word quickly spread. Although several newspapers and trade publications detailed the highlights of his life, one tribute came from a publication close to Howard's heart.

The *Milling & Baking News* told its readers:

> *Howard S. Holmes, retired chairman of Chelsea Milling Co., died Jan. 3. He was 87.*
>
> *Together with his twin brother, Dudley, and his mother, Mabel, Mr. Holmes began running Chelsea Milling in 1936 upon the death of his father. The company thrived under his leadership, building its unique niche in the manufacture of the Jiffy brand of consumer mixes. Chelsea Milling said the Holmes family launched Jiffy Mixes 69 years ago when Howard's mother invented the nation's first retail prepared mix. According to the company, Ms. Holmes said, "The mix is so simple even a man can do it."*
>
> *With a family history in milling dating back to 1802, Mr. Holmes and his brother represented the eighth generation of millers. In his characteristic humorous and self-deprecating style, Mr. Holmes said, "It just goes to show you what idiots we are. We're too dumb to get out of the business."*
>
> *Active in industry activities, Mr. Holmes was chairman of the Millers' National Federation from 1970 to 1972 and was a director until 1996. In October 2000, he was elected an honorary member of the North American Millers' Association, the successor group to the M.N.F.*
>
> *Active in the corporate and civic worlds, Mr. Holmes sat on the boards of directors of Domino's Pizza, the Mennel Milling Co., Chelsea State Bank, the Ronald McDonald House and Boy Scouts of America.*
>
> *Mr. Holmes attended Chelsea public schools; Phillips Exeter Academy, Exeter, N.H.; and Princeton University, Princeton, N.J. He was awarded a B.S. in mechanical engineering from the University of Michigan.*

Howdy's Tribute to his Father

Mom, Family Members, Team Jiffy, Friends of Dad, and Respectful Guests—

Thank you so much for being here. . . . As you know, Dad was never comfortable with recognition. He is here today, and wonders what everyone is doing up so early.

Dad was all about giving and sharing.

It is appropriate to mention that he always consulted and received encouragement and direction from his partner, Tiny. What an incredible team they were.

Dad was very fond of animals, especially dogs. He was our "top dog."

Dad loved people. He was a skilled communicator. He always enjoyed kidding with the ladies.

For the past twelve years, I've had the honor to be with Dad every day at the office. He loved his work so much. He really enjoyed being in the plant and talking with people. He looked forward each day to interacting with our employees and respected them very much.

This year in April, Chelsea Milling Company celebrates our 100th anniversary. The legacy Dad has created is unparalleled. We believe in certain principles, treat each other with respect, and always try to do the right thing.

What did Howard teach us? In his actions, he showed us how to be fair with others. He was respectful of people. He taught us how to live in the moment. He always put others first. He showed us that having a good sense of humor puts others at ease. He was a class guy.

The qualities I'll always cherish the most are his smile and that ever-ready twinkle in his eye. He made everyone feel special. When he felt a little underappreciated within the family, he would say, "I'll go on."

Well, Dad, now you have gone on. We love you so very much. You are my hero.

Mr. Holmes is survived by his wife of 55 years, Mary (Tiny) Blodgett Holmes; his brother, Dudley; and five children, including Howard S. (Howdy) Holmes, current president and CEO of Chelsea Milling Company.

When June Robinson, Howard's secretary of forty-some years, received the phone call she'd been dreading, she flew home from Florida for the funeral. She wasn't the only one who traveled great distances to pay last respects to Howard. On January 8, the First Presbyterian Church of Ann Arbor was filled to bursting with friends, business associates, and employees.

Howard Sumner Holmes' devotion to the noblest principles of living and his unfailing generosity with his time were qualities for which he will long be remembered with great affection.

1913 - 2001

A PLAQUE COMMEMORATING HOWARD'S LIFE AT CHELSEA MILLING GREETS VISITORS LEAVING THE MAIN OFFICE.

HOWARD SUMNER HOLMES
1913-2001

"It's strange how many of my father's phrases I've adopted since he died," Howdy said several years later. "He often affectionately referred to people as 'knuckleheads,' and I use that expression, too. One of the sincerest compliments I received happened at my father's funeral, when some of the gals in the packaging department told me it would be all right with them if I called them 'monsters,' like Dad did."

In their later years, both of the twins suffered from memory loss. Dudley Sr.'s daughter Diane reported that for more than a year after Howard's funeral, "for what seemed like the thousandth time," Dudley said, "I haven't seen Howard today." Diane said it was very hard on him, "Every time someone told him that Howard was gone, it was like he was hearing it for the first time."

Dudley's failing memory was diagnosed as senile dementia rather than Alzheimer's disease, and it progressed more gradually than his brother's. Dudley's wife, Nancy, had died in June 1990. Until the summer of 2002, Dudley was able to live alone, with daily visits from a caregiver, in the large house that his grandfather built on East Middle Street, the same house where Mabel White Holmes had developed the JIFFY Biscuit Mix.

Dudley worked hard to thwart his family's efforts to move him to the retirement home in Chelsea. Dudley had slept in the same house all his life, and he wasn't going to live anywhere else if he could help it. Twice he managed to evade nurses at the retirement home late at night and walked over a mile back to his empty house. Police found him both times sound asleep in his bed, his clothing folded neatly nearby. In fall 2002, however, a stumble and fall left Dudley disabled and disoriented. After hospitalization, his family moved him permanently to the Alzheimer's facility where his brother had died a year earlier.

The year 2003 was another difficult and sad time for the Holmes family and Chelsea Milling's employees. Mary "Tiny" Blodgett Holmes died in August, and Dudley followed five weeks later, on September 22.

"It's the end of an era—for Chelsea as well as for us," company employee Anna Louise Knickerbocker said sadly at the time. "There has always been a Holmes living in that big gray house, and there has always been a twin somewhere around this plant, as long as anyone can remember."

Chelsea Standard
September 29, 2003

Dudley Kirke Holmes, 90, of Chelsea, died Sept. 22, 2003, at the United Methodist Retirement Community. He was born July 24, 1913, in Chelsea, the son of Howard Samuel and Mabel White Holmes.

He married Nancy Muir Brown in San Francisco, Calif., on June 14, 1941. She preceded him in death on June 30, 1990.

Beloved and devoted husband and father, he is survived by one son, Dudley K. Holmes Jr. (Dawn) of Chelsea; two daughters, Diane (Robert) Hall of East Grand Rapids and Susan (Kim) Schrotenboer of Ada, nine grandchildren; and one great-grandchild.

He was preceded in death by his twin brother, Howard S. Holmes, in 2001.

Mr. Holmes graduated from Chelsea High School and Phillips Exeter Academy. He received a bachelor's degree from the University of Michigan in 1936, and went to serve his country as a lieutenant in the U.S. Navy during World War II in the South Pacific.

Mr. Holmes served as vice president of the Chelsea Milling Co. He and his wife, Nancy, developed and perfected the vast majority of formulas for Jiffy Mixes in their family kitchen on East Middle Street.

Mr. Holmes lived his entire life in Chelsea, where he was deeply involved in the community. He served on the board of trustees of the Chelsea School District, the board of directors of the Chelsea State Bank, and the Chelsea Community Hospital.

Mr. Holmes was also a member of the Kiwanis Club and a founding member of the Cultural Club…

A private burial will follow at Oak Grove Cemetery.

DUDLEY KIRKE HOLMES
1913-2003

HOWDY'S FATHER AND GRANDFATHER BOTH RAN A SOLE PROPRIETORSHIP. HOWDY INTRODUCED
AN INTERDEPENDENT MANAGEMENT SYSTEM TO CHELSEA MILLING THAT WAS WELL
UNDER WAY BY THE END OF THE TWENTIETH CENTURY.

Values and Business Practices
Rolling the Mill into the Twenty-First Century

Howdy stood in the company's boardroom and explained to a group of his administrators, "There are basically three different management styles, the sole proprietorship, the hierarchy, and the interdependent method.

"Sole proprietorship is spelled S-O-L-E, but it might as well be spelled S-O-U-L because that's what goes into the business: an individual's soul and heart," he continued. He drew a pyramid to represent a sole proprietorship and said, "This is usually the form a first-generation business takes. There is a very small management team on top, and the majority of workers are lumped together on the bottom, all reporting to the owner. This system has little or no delegation of authority." His father ran a sole proprietorship, Howdy pointed out. Longtime employees nodded their heads in agreement.

"The second form of management, a business hierarchy, can be illustrated with a series of boxes connected with solid or dotted lines that ultimately—and sometimes circuitously—lead to the one box at the top," Howdy said, picking up his marker once again to draw the configuration. "Although this is the management style adopted by most corporations, this system often grows unwieldy because there is too much delegation of responsibilities and decision-making," he continued, as he finished drawing the interconnected boxes. "People in a system like this can hide behind screens. Messages become diluted as they filter down the ladder.

"The third—and most difficult management form to accomplish—is the interdependent management system," said Howdy. "Another term for this style is teaming—here, there is no boss to hide behind or defer to. The interdependent management system is difficult to sell to people who are used to the other, more traditional, management styles. Interdependence is difficult to achieve, in function as well as in practice. At first, people fear being exposed. Interdependence requires the participants to trust each other—and trust doesn't come easily. That's something that is earned. This management style requires a lot of effort." Howdy paused, scanned his audience, and said, "This is the style I've been introducing to Chelsea Milling over the past fifteen years."

In a different meeting, this one with prospective employees, Howdy explained that the Chelsea Milling culture is "a mixture of nineteenth-century values and twenty-first-century business practices" and that it "is different from just about any other business setting.

"I consider anything outside of Chelsea Milling as the 'Real World,'" he told them, with a spark of humor in his eye. "People who come here have developed practices and beliefs that are a product of Real World cultures—and most of the time those practices and procedures are much more brutal than what we choose to have here. The Chelsea Milling Company culture is about teaming, openness, and interdependence. People who join this company have to recalibrate themselves to our belief system. We have to get 'the poison' out of them. After they're hired, they want to start adding value right away, but we want our new people to wait and figure out who we are and how we operate. We always urge them to 'detox' for awhile."

Forbes magazine in its 2001 article echoed this patient philosophy in their interview with Howdy:

> Holmes, sensitive to his family's heritage and his father's reign, repeatedly stresses that he still respects the firm's old way of doing things and that he has made changes incrementally, not overnight. [Jack] Kennedy, the general manager [now vice president and general manager], says Holmes' patient but persistent approach allowed the newcomers to settle into their roles. "It's natural for a person coming in from an outside company to want to contribute right away, to want to do something heroic. But that is not what this organization wants—they want us to step back and spend our time worrying about relationships and culture and adapting. Then there will be plenty of time for contributions."

The system apparently works very well. The *Forbes* article went on to inform readers that the reason for the company's success is that it is privately held, "which gives it the freedom to be fast on its feet." If change is perceived as necessary, it is implemented quickly. "We're not tied to analysts' expectations on gross profit margins," Howdy explained in the article. "We can make pricing decisions based solely on what makes sense, not on shareholder demands."

Another reason for the company's success is its streamlined approach to decision-making and manufacturing. Chelsea Milling dispenses with corporate bureaucracy in favor of efficiency. In a larger corporation, decision-making is far more complicated, filtered through three or four departments before implementation. At Chelsea Milling, three or four people at a time are the maximum involved in making a decision. Of the company's 350 employees,

"The Chelsea Milling Company culture is about teaming, openness, and interdependence. People who join this company have to recalibrate themselves to our belief system. We have to get 'the poison' out of them."

the majority of them work in manufacturing. The company is almost entirely self-sufficient. It stores its own flour, grinds its own grain, and shrink-wraps packages on-site. Everything is done on-site with the exception of the blue and white boxes, which are printed forty-five miles west of Chelsea by a company that Chelsea Milling also owns.

JIFFY's national competitors are General Mills and Pillsbury; regional competitors include Martha White, Washington Brand Mixes, and Krusteaz. At one time, the big national corporations also used to mill and package their own product just like JIFFY does, but over the years these companies decided the overhead was excessive, so they sold their mills and storage facilities and turned to others for those services. Chelsea Milling, however, still does everything the old-fashioned way, "from milling flour to mixing, packaging, warehousing, and shipping. This way, we can control the quality of everything we do, and there isn't an upcharge for outsourcing any services," said Howdy.

Howdy has long recognized the similarities between racing and running a corporation. "Racing is calculated risk-taking. So is business," he said. "Although race car drivers take risks, they're not risk-takers. The idea isn't to splatter yourself against a wall, it's to see how you can respond to challenge and instant decision-making. You have to develop a focus, sort out stimuli, and make good decisions," Howdy continued. "To me, the pleasure comes in testing the degree to which I can push my own envelope. That was true when I was in racing, and it is equally true in the business world."

When a decision to change has been necessary, Howdy has relied on his training in the racing world. "On the mechanical side, race cars require consistency to enhance performance. So does a manufacturing facility," he said. "If a racing team doesn't pay close attention to maintenance and documentation, there could be trouble. The same holds true for manufacturers. Racing is utterly interdependent; a team of people work to get—and keep—the car in the race. We promote this interdependent team concept of management at Chelsea Milling."

"I would call Howdy's management style cautiously aggressive," said Jack Kennedy. "Howdy has great vision. His plans are well thought out. He's a student of business and management, and he carefully considers his moves. He has the ability to stay focused on the core values of the business," according to Kennedy. "Howdy saw the need for an interdependent decision-making process, and we all work as a team to make this company work."

Howdy has identified a handful of core principles that he believes have been responsible for the company's longevity. The first is a commitment to giving "Mrs. Smith"—the name that represents every consumer everywhere—quality and value for her money. Another is a commitment to making the mill a safe, clean, encouraging environment for the people working there. "Those core principles filled the treasure box of what we wouldn't—couldn't—let go of. Everything else, I felt, was subject to evaluation," Howdy said.

The decisions Howdy eventually made after careful consideration included modernizing a manufacturing schedule that suffered from outdated machinery and relied very heavily on overtime. Howdy also approved a preventive maintenance program—"incredibly, the company's first," *Forbes* noted—for the aging packaging equipment. These changes took place as the physical plant went through a major modernization campaign. The number of production lines rose from thirteen to seventeen, the quality-control mechanisms were upgraded from analog to electronic, a new 125,000-square-foot warehouse was constructed that was capable of storing more than a million cases of JIFFY. Thanks to these changes, production capacity rose by 40 percent, and the facility now has the capability of producing 1.6 million boxes daily. These improvements not only ended boom-bust production cycles and their resulting need for overtime, but also provide a launching pad for further sales growth.

Another decision, perhaps symbolic of the new management's commitment to safety and efficiency, was to tear down three outdated and unused 1930s-era grain silos. One of them was the silo in which Howdy's grandfather, the first Howard S. Holmes, had fallen to his death.

AFTER HOWDY TOOK THE REINS OF THE COMPANY, THE PHYSICAL PLANT WENT THROUGH A MAJOR MODERNIZATION CAMPAIGN. THE NUMBER OF PRODUCTION LINES ROSE FROM THIRTEEN TO SEVENTEEN, THE QUALITY-CONTROL MECHANISMS WERE UPGRADED FROM ANALOG TO ELECTRONIC, AND A NEW 125,000-SQUARE-FOOT WAREHOUSE WAS CONSTRUCTED THAT WAS CAPABLE OF STORING MORE THAN A MILLION CASES OF JIFFY.

Although the Chelsea Milling Company is poised to meet future demands, the market is constantly changing. The company's biggest challenge—the American consumer—remains out of the company's control. Beginning back in the 1990s, the dry-mix market slowly began shrinking as the dizzying pace of modern life began to redefine the notion of a convenience product. Americans were rapidly changing baking traditions, eating habits, and shopping routines. Dry mixes were now suddenly competing head to head with ready-made, prepared, and frozen foods.

Howdy addressed the changing market in his interview with *Forbes*:

> *Holmes says one thing not in the offing is selling the brand, although he claims there have been several offers. ("We consider it very flattering,*

but no, thanks.") With JIFFY sales growing despite the tightening
market, and the company carrying no debt, Holmes feels Chelsea Milling
is well positioned to make adjustments, several of which he's already
considering. "Right now we're just in the retail market, but we are
seriously looking at export. We are seriously looking at institutional. We
are seriously looking at food service. All these are possibilities."

Although the Holmes family will never sell the mill, the family may consider making some purchases of their own; new acquisitions are also a possibility, Howdy acknowledged. Howdy's office often showcases an array of competitors' products and related food items for the president and his staff to study and discuss.

Howdy's wife, Carole, does her own competitive market research, which she passes on to her husband. She admitted to conducting informal surveys on her visits to supermarkets. "I love watching people, observing what they buy and how they make their choices," she said. "I've studied women's shopping habits since the days when I was pushing my baby in the shopping cart. I always talk to shoppers, asking their views, suggesting that they try one of our muffin flavors, or asking what they think about other packaged products." She also buys competitors' products to make comparisons to JIFFY. "I get my hands in the mixes and feel the textures. I evaluate the frostings—too sugary? creamy enough? too dry? any aftertaste? I troubleshoot. And, by the way, my cupboards are full of JIFFY!"

The gap between Chelsea Milling and its competitors is ever-widening. While many of its competitors have been sold to multinational corporations, Chelsea Milling remains a privately held family business. And, while prices for competitors' products have soared, a box of JIFFY muffin mix still costs less than a candy bar. The old-fashioned sales decisions that JIFFY's founders established in the 1930s have over time come to be considered revolutionary. Production costs are kept as low as possible. The focus remains on "Mrs. Smith" and not the bottom profit line. And, as was the case in Howard's day, no money is spent on advertising or coupons. Instead, JIFFY relies on word of mouth—"and there is a pun attached to that statement," Howdy said with a grin. "A personal endorsement is worth more than a coupon or

fancy slogan any day." It is a source of pride to Howdy that his sales force won't cut deals for larger customers. "Whether you buy 100,000 cases or one, the price is the same," he said firmly. "We offer no volume discounts or bracket pricing. We don't want our list price to be different in Kansas City than in Spokane or Boston. Our bottom-line consideration is the consumer. Really."

Jack Kennedy listed the ways that the company has adapted its solid, old-fashioned philosophies to meet current demands: "We try to make ourselves very easy to deal with, both internally and with customers. We try to keep the work force very stable. We do a lot of repairs and projects in-house. Logistics are crucial. We must be very efficient to service our customers, and we try to offer top-quality service. That's the way this family has chosen to do business through the generations. Howdy's got a lot of souls—employees, family members, and consumers—for whom he feels a deep sense of responsibility."

Like his father, his grandfather, and great-grandfather before him, Howdy hires people based on character, not on slick job resumes. "You can teach anyone tasks, but you can't teach character, integrity, principles, and conscience," he said. "Those are the important things. One hundred times out of one hundred, if you have a person with unwavering character, the tasks will be done very well.

"We spend most of our management time on the 'soft skills,' the people-oriented and growth-enhancing skills," said Howdy. He launched a continuing education program shortly after taking over as CEO and began budgeting for training and skills development programs. The company assists employees with the cost of degree programs from local colleges and universities. Howdy's commitment to people is more than a company slogan, but in case you need to see it in print, a sign on the CEO's office door reads:

"The mission of Team Jiffy is to achieve 100% product integrity with quality people caring about each other."

Next to that is the Thought for the Day:

"Never be afraid to try something new.
Remember, amateurs built the ark, professionals built the Titanic."

Shortly after taking the reins of the company, Howdy coined the term "Jiffyville" to further enhance the community feeling within Chelsea Milling. He also promoted the visual of a train leaving the station at Jiffyville and heading into a new future. "I like to think of our business as a community made up of all kinds of people: firemen, protesters, activists, cooks, drivers, thinkers, planners," he said. "What I'm trying to do with the Jiffyville analogy is to enhance our quality of life, to encourage everyone to be nice to people, and to treat them like good neighbors, which is something that the people here have always traditionally done."

In summer 2002 Howdy had a huge mural of the JIFFY Corn Muffin Mix box painted on the side of the bran and midds storage tower. "I had to figure out how to be helpful to the community in a dramatic

and visible way. This was part of the answer," he explained. "In some
ways, the milling company has put Chelsea on the nation's map. When
Chelsea residents go somewhere else and talk about their hometown,
they mention, 'It's where the JIFFY products are made.' The mural idea
visibly connects Chelsea with JIFFY. It wasn't a brilliant marketing idea.
One day I just looked at the tower and from one direction it looked
like a box. I suddenly wondered why we didn't use our goodwill and
nationally known products to promote the city of Chelsea and tie it

JIFFY'S TOWER MURAL, DEPICTING THE NATION'S FAVORITE MUFFIN MIX, STANDS IN THE CENTER OF TOWN. IT HAS BECOME CHELSEA'S MOST FAMOUS LANDMARK.

even more closely with JIFFY."

When employee Anna Louise Knickerbocker read the *Ann Arbor News* story about Howdy's idea to paint that mural, she was pleased. "Howdy is a good public relations man," she said. "His family has done a lot for the town, though most of it hasn't been publicized. They've been good at giving back to the place that has been good to them."

THE PACKAGING LINE AT JIFFY IS A CONTINUOUS RIBBON OF BLUE AND WHITE BOXES.

A Tour of "Jiffyville"
The Mill and the Office, Past and Present

Between sixteen- and eighteen-thousand people tour the Chelsea Milling Company each year. On a weekday morning, guide Lynne Roskowski-Farley ushered tour groups into a viewing room, where a slide show telling the company's history was followed by samples of JIFFY's fresh baked goods. Chelsea Milling currently makes twenty-two retail products and one food service product, including mixes for muffins, cakes, brownies, frosting, pancakes, pizza crust, pie crust, and all-purpose baking mixes.

Roskowski-Farley has worked at Chelsea Milling for twenty-two years, following in her mother's footsteps. "My mother was here for about twenty years," she said. "I've stayed because I like the feel of the old-fashioned family business."

Her visitors finished the samples and all donned hair nets. Roskowski-Farley took them on a tour through the facility, starting at the packaging line. In its 2003 article "Do You Know the Muffin Man?" the *Chelsea Standard* wrote: "Jiffyville even has a 'roller coaster.' It will never rival the thrill rides at amusement parks, but people don't ride it—boxes of Jiffy Mix do." The roller coaster is a continuous ribbon of blue and white boxes traveling a distance of eight to nine miles from the box-filling station to eventual consolidation into cartons. The line starts with empty boxes that are pulled onto conveyors by suction cups, opened, inserted with liners, and filled with the appropriate mix of Michigan wheat and other ingredients. Chelsea Milling uses two and a half million bushels of flour each year, held in twenty-seven on-site silos.

A typical tour ends in the corn muffin room, where visitors are given their own boxes of JIFFY Mix and a recipe book. As they leave through the loading dock door, visitors can watch trucks being packed with boxes—more than a million a day—bound for grocery stores and supermarkets across the country. JIFFY Corn Muffin Mix is the seventh-best-selling dry grocery item in the country, controlling 88 percent of its market.

A private tour of the mill reveals a richer picture of what really goes into making the fillings for those little blue and white boxes. Although the milling process still generates basically the same products that it did hundreds of years ago, Chelsea Milling's current technology is as modern as today's computerized systems allow. Gone is the steam engine that once was used to turn the grindstone, and gone is the grindstone itself. Gone too are the farmers who used to exchange news in the mill as they watched their grain being ground into flour. And although there's still plenty of news exchanged on the floor of Chelsea Milling, now the mill is occupied by a staff of white-clad, computer-savvy technicians who run a multi-story, high-tech complex of rollers and sifters.

Wes Lentz stood in the control room of the technologically advanced mill, scanning computer screens to assess how much flour is in storage and determine the efficiency of each roller-sifter assembly line. A native of Kansas, Lentz grew up on a farm that raised wheat, corn, sorghum, and cattle. He arrived in Chelsea in 1997. His career in flour milling began twenty-one years earlier, in 1976—"August 18, to be exact"—when he began sweeping floors for Pillsbury in Atchison, Kansas. Always dressed in white, with hair net squarely in place, Lentz supervises everything associated with the general efficiency of the mill, including the grain elevators and the feed tower where the feed is stored and processed. Residual products from the milling process—bran and middlings—are always recycled, never wasted. The bran is sold to cereal companies, and the middlings are sold for animal feed.

These days, the milling process starts when wheat is delivered by truck and unloaded into silos, then transferred from silos into a bin on top of the mill. "First, we clean and prepare the grain by running it through a series of machines to remove all the foreign materials—for example, corn kernels, leaves, debris from the field," said Lentz. "Then we clean it, scour it, and temper it."

The cleaning and scouring processes require between five and ten minutes. The tempering process is longer. After water is added, it takes approximately twelve hours to complete the tempering cycle. Computers determine the degree of moisture in the wheat and then water is added to bring the wheat up to optimal milling moisture. This helps separate the outer coat of bran from the white heart inside the wheat berry, so

WHEN THE MILL OPERATES AT FULL CAPACITY, IT CAN PROCESS 9,000 BUSHELS OF WHEAT A DAY OR 420,000 POUNDS OF FLOUR. MIXING DEPARTMENT EMPLOYEE AL SCHAUER MONITORS AND ADDS INGREDIENTS TO A BATCH OF CORN MUFFIN MIX.

that only the wheat berry will be ground. "We don't want to grind the bran. The whiter the flour, the better its quality," explained Lentz. Each kernel of wheat that enters the mill will be run up and down through the milling process between twenty and forty times. This process, which involves a gradual reduction of the kernel of wheat, takes about twenty minutes or so to run its course.

During the milling process, the kernels of wheat will go through many different machines. On the first floor of the mill, three rows of roller mills stand in military precision, each containing two pairs of heavy metal rollers. The bottom roller revolves at a different speed from the top roller, creating the action that will separate the heart of the

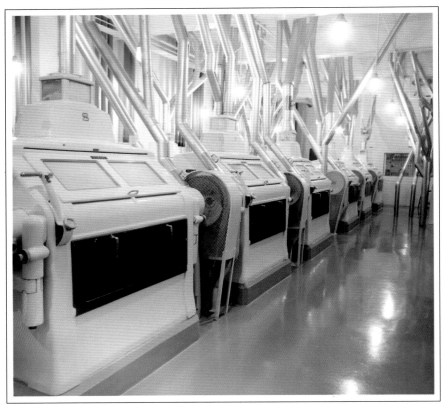

"Every machine is different; they're all set up for a different process," explained miller Wes Lentz. Shown above are roller mills used to process wheat into flour.

berry from the bran. "Every machine is different; they're all set up for a different process," Lentz said. After the roller mills, large shaking boxes called sifters sift out the flour and send it to the storage bin.

Chelsea Milling's flour mill produces two types of flour for its baking products: biscuit flour and type A, or straight, flour. Years ago, the mill also processed cake flour, but that is now purchased from other mills. The flour mill can store 5,000 bushels of wheat and 1.6 million pounds of flour. The elevators store an additional 1 million bushels. When the mill operates at full capacity for twenty-four-hour stretches, it can process 9,000 bushels of wheat a day. That amounts to 420,000 pounds of flour each day. Computer monitors show the current storage of flour within each of the bins.

In the 1960s, Chelsea Milling abandoned the business of selling flour wholesale and devoted itself exclusively to JIFFY products. "We're busy running to keep up with our own business," said Lentz. "This is a very high-maintenance operation. We have a complete schedule of cleaning, repairing, changing filter bags, and repainting, to keep everything running at peak efficiency."

Dudley Holmes Jr. retired from his position at the mill in June 2003, after thirty-four years on the job. He was the first member of the family's fourth generation to work there. Dudley grew up in Chelsea, in the home that Harmon S. Holmes built on East Middle Street. After graduating from Hope College and traveling around the world, he joined the family business in 1969, when Chelsea Milling had ten production lines and about 180 employees; at the time he left, the plant had seventeen lines and 350 employees.

Dudley learned, after taking over his father's position at the mill, that purchasing raw ingredients is a rigorous job requiring knowledge of the weather, national politics, and international affairs.

On a day in 2000 Dudley was on the phone in his office talking to a wheat supplier. "You have a total of 8,000 bushels?" Dudley said to the person on the other end of the line. "I can pay $4.15 for it. With storage charges, we'd probably pay $4.30. The $4.15 price is only good for today, so you'll have to get back to me."

Off the phone, Dudley continued, "This business is fun. I wheel and deal to get us the best prices. When we're in the midst of the wheat harvest, I get those calls all the time. Farmers are shopping around for the best price. Before the harvest is over, Chelsea Milling will have 900,000 bushels of wheat stored here on the premises, and I'll have already arranged for shipments in January, February, and March." Major price changes can occur almost overnight. "Buying wheat is like a roll of the dice. I do a lot of reading to be able to anticipate what's happening to the products we need to buy," Dudley said. "This is a business where you have to be on top of all that's happening."

Back in 1969, wheat was selling for between $1.50 and $2.50 per bushel; in 2003, the year Dudley retired, the price was $4.15, and farmers had become much more efficient at growing wheat. The same acre that raised twenty-five bushels in 1969 now produced seventy bushels. In 1969, the old silos stored 100,000 bushels of wheat; the new silos hold 900,000 bushels. Until the 1970s, Chelsea Milling relied on the railroad for shipments; now all raw materials arrive by truck, and only bran and middlings leave by train.

"When I came, I knew I should learn everything there is about the Chelsea Milling Company, but I won't deny that it was difficult," Dudley said during that 2000 interview, as he glanced out his office window and back through the years. "I think that people wanted to see the boss's son make some mistakes." He spent a year working in each department at the mill. He learned how to mix product, run machinery, and do "just about everything else."

When Walter Scott retired as plant manager, Dudley was put in charge of purchasing all corrugated boxes for bulk packaging. The man who sold Chelsea Milling its boxes, Dan Staelgraeve, came to Dudley suggesting that Chelsea Milling make and print its own corrugated boxes. That was the start of C&S (Chelsea and Stoner) Carton. Howard built the Marshall, Michigan, plant that Hank Stoner ran for many years. Blank cardboard is cut and printed there as well, to make the trademark JIFFY boxes.

At the time Dudley Sr. decided to retire as vice president of purchasing in 1984, Dudley Jr. had limited purchasing experience and no training. "Howard felt it was too much responsibility for me, but the day when I discovered we only had 10,000 bushels of wheat left at the mill—and we used 35,000 or 40,000 bushels a week—I began to work my way into this position," Dudley Jr. recalled.

His job required constant reading, cloud watching, and study. "The weather plays a great part in our business," Dudley explained. "South America grows soy and corn, so I have to pay attention to what's happening in South America, weather-wise and politically. Cocoa comes from Africa, the Ivory Coast, and about every two weeks, it seems, there's a new political crisis that can affect shipment of products. Bananas arrive from Costa Rica. If a hurricane hits Costa Rica, we may have to look for new suppliers instantly. Salt comes from Cargill in St. Clair [Michigan]; we need to know when canning season starts because Heinz and Vlasic also buy their salt from Cargill. Before canning season, we have to store our salt supply for two months if

DUDLEY HOLMES JR. SOON LEARNED THAT PURCHASING RAW INGREDIENTS IS A RIGOROUS JOB, REQUIRING KNOWLEDGE OF WEATHER, POLITICS, AND INTERNATIONAL AFFAIRS.

we're to have enough for our needs."

Dudley's greatest challenge, however, was to balance the quantity and price of wheat. Chelsea Milling uses hundreds of thousands of bushels of wheat every quarter. Local farmers have not been growing wheat for many years now, so Dudley had to go farther afield to keep the flour mill operating.

Every year, Dudley would buy millions of pounds of cornmeal, sugar, baking soda, salt, vegetable shortening, and lard—not to mention hundreds of thousands of pounds of icing sugar. Every day, ten or twelve trucks rumbled through town, delivering different JIFFY ingredients

"WE WERE RECYCLING BEFORE ANYONE ELSE KNEW ABOUT THE BENEFITS OF RECYCLING,"
SAID DUDLEY HOLMES JR. EACH YEAR JIFFY RECYCLES AN AVERAGE OF 400,000
POUNDS OF PAPER AND CORRUGATED BOXES.

(this is still true today). Chelsea Milling primarily uses beet sugar from the Thumb area of Michigan and North Dakota's Red River Valley. "The freight for bringing cane sugar up from Florida or Alabama makes beet sugar a better option for us," Dudley said. "There's no difference in flavor between the two sugars, though cane sugar is a little finer."

Dudley's job never focused entirely on purchasing, however. He is proud of his work with Wayne Ruggles to create the machine room where Chelsea Milling makes its own replacement parts. The packaging machines are ancient, and parts for them no longer exist. The original manufacturer kept the drawings and offered to make the parts, but

Dudley decided that the set-up charges would be exorbitant. If Chelsea Milling needed a crankshaft—and all the machines need a replacement crankshaft over time—the manufacturer would have charged $12,000; Ruggles calculated that his machinists could make it for $2,000. Dudley decided to take the $10,000 difference and invest it in machinery. Ruggles made the mechanical drawings of every part of machinery Chelsea Milling would need, and in the mid-1980s the company's machinists began making parts.

The milling industry is a natural for the promotion of recycling, and it became a personal interest of Dudley's. Throughout its history, Chelsea Milling has recycled the by-products of milling. "Our facilities can hold 180,000 pounds of bran, and bran takes up a lot of space, so with the kind of turnaround we have, cereal companies get very fresh bran from us," Dudley explained. He took recycling several steps further. "We were recycling before anyone else knew about the benefits of recycling," he said. "It was a way to save money—and, equally important, it was a way to help the environment." One of his accomplishments made industry news. In 1992 Susan Lutzow wrote in *Bakery Mart*:

> *Dudley Holmes combines personal convictions with definitive actions.*
>
> *Holmes, v.p. of manufacturing for Chelsea Milling Co., had been horrified by the amount of bulk-paper waste his Chelsea, Michigan-based company was generating to landfills every year. He set out to remedy the situation.*
>
> *He soon realized, however, that it would not be easy. That's because a good portion of the waste was from the bags used to store sodium bicarbonate, a vital ingredient to the company's operation. Highly absorbent, sodium bicarbonate has a tendency to cake during storage. To prevent caking, manufacturers normally package it in plastic-lined paper bags.*
>
> *These bags, unfortunately, cannot be recycled, and are always dumped in landfills. . . .*
>
> *Because sodium bicarbonate is such an integral part of Chelsea Milling's baking mix product line, Holmes deduced that the ingredient*

itself couldn't change. Rather, its storage container must. . . .

What Holmes discovered was that Church & Dwight had begun developing . . . a brand of sodium bicarbonate that could be stored in recyclable plastic bags. The company added a high-performance flow agent to its ARM & HAMMER sodium bicarbonate. . . .

Holmes explains that he is not only helping the environment, but that he is also saving his company money. . . . He has begun requesting recyclable bags for other ingredients.

But there was even better news from the recycling project. "The icing on the cake is that the local paper company in Chelsea actually pays us for the bags," Dudley said. "They recycle and re-use them to create other paper products."

Sanitation also became Dudley's concern. Traditionally, every Fourth of July weekend Chelsea Milling would fumigate the plant, but the fumigation was haphazard and chemicals would leak out of the old building. Dudley became certified to handle restricted-use pesticides; he introduced a powerful vacuum system and a policy of constant vacuuming. Nowadays, pesticides are only a last, and seldom-used, resort.

In 2003, the year Dudley retired, Chelsea Milling built three new silos for cornmeal, ensuring a one-week supply. "For years we had been going hand-to-mouth with cornmeal," Dudley said at the time. "Until the new silos, what was delivered one day was used the next; if a truck broke down, we were in trouble." One of his final tasks for the company was to investigate whether it should turn back the clock and return to receiving shipments of cornmeal by rail.

As he began to train his replacement, Ed Hostetter, in December 2002, Dudley contemplated the past and the future of the family business. "I used to know everyone here, their husbands, wives, dogs and cats, but the company has become so big that it's no longer possible. So much change has come, and change will continue to come. The automation that's taken place is incredible—everything is computer-driven. I'm a victim of the pencil and paper; I can do what I do without a computer (although I use one, reluctantly). There is a lot of talk about allergen labeling; ninety percent of Americans are allergic to something. That could have an impact on us in coming years. The future holds some interesting challenges."

"OUR JOB IS NOT TO PROVIDE THE CHEAPEST VALUE, BUT THE BEST VALUE," EXPLAINED
VICE PRESIDENT AND GENERAL MANAGER JACK KENNEDY.

One day in 2002 Jack Kennedy checked the computer screen in his office, signed a requisition slip, then leaned forward in his office chair and said, "Our purpose was defined by Howard Holmes long ago, when he said, 'You've got to give Mrs. Smith value for her money.' In Howard's mind, Mrs. Smith was every consumer, and value meant offering quality at a good cost. That's my job, in a nutshell. Our job is not to provide the *cheapest* value, but the *best* value." To do this, Kennedy's operation relies on another business policy Howard established more than a half-century ago: controlling costs so the savings can be passed on to the consumer. "We try to make decisions wisely," said Kennedy, "with a great deal of forethought."

EVERY DAY JIFFY TRUCKS RUMBLE THROUGH TOWN, RETURNING FROM DELIVERING
JIFFY MIXES TO NEIGHBORING STATES.

Kennedy came to Chelsea Milling as director of operations in 1995, after working for two very large farmers' co-ops: Ocean Spray Cranberry and Welch's. He soon learned that his job is like a three-legged stool, with plant superintendent (processing and packaging), logistics manager (supervising the warehouse, shipping and receiving), and plant engineer (supervising maintenance and projects) being the legs. Howdy hired Kennedy to bring the three legs of operations into a new age. "The company required a lot of work because there hadn't been much capital investment in years," said Kennedy. In 1995, the plant was running seventeen product lines twenty-four hours a day, seven days a week, with machinery dating back to the 1950s and 1960s that had been retrofitted and well maintained.

Changes aren't made without a great deal of care, and planning, Kennedy learned. "Any changes here have to be appropriate to the traditions established a long time ago," he said. "The philosophy is not to choose the newest thing out on the market, but to optimize the use of what we have. The basic truth is that the amount going into Americans' stomachs hasn't changed over time. We just need to be adaptable enough to maintain or increase our share of that consumption."

Kennedy soon learned that the company had no reason for a blistering pace. "We have the luxury of making changes at our own pace, not out of necessity. This business is loaded with opportunities," he said. "The trick is that as we make change, we take advantage of opportunities very carefully. Since the business is so healthy, we have the luxury to really think through changes before we need to implement anything."

Together with Douglas Tomney and Howdy, Kennedy created a capital expenditure policy and began to make systematic improvements. In 1996, Chelsea Milling added a new warehouse. In 2000 the company tore down its old silos. That year plans were under way to modernize the mixing department. Testing of new state-of-the-art technology designed to fit the mixing lines perfectly resulted in a rise in the production rate from 100 to 160 boxes per minute. Mix accuracies were reduced from ten grams down to accuracy at measurements of one gram. Although wet chemistry remained the backup, product testing had come a long way from the days when test kitchen supervisor Phyllis Stepp had to bake something from every line; today the testing relies on very sophisticated computer analysis. "We're working our way through forty-four projects that have been approved for this year [2002], as well as thirty currently under way," said Kennedy.

In 2002 chief financial officer Douglas Tomney scanned a long row of figures on his computer screen, then turned and pointed to an old-fashioned executive ledger with numbers written in neat, tiny script. "This is the way bookkeeping was done when I arrived in 1993," Tomney said. "I would have to ask Howard if I could borrow the ledger—and even then he always asked why."

In 1991, director of sales Bernie Schipper became the first nonfamily member on the management team; two years later, Tomney became the second. His path to Chelsea Milling was a circuitous one. Scottish by birth, he served an apprenticeship as an accountant while attending Glasgow University. He and his wife left Scotland in 1967, spent three years in Jamaica and three in Montreal, and then joined a company that took them to Cedar Rapids, Iowa. There he joined National Oats, a

DOUGLAS TOMNEY WITH HOWDY.

division of Curtice Burns Foods, as vice president of finance. While he was at National Oats, an executive recruiter called to tell him about an opening at Chelsea Milling for chief financial officer. Tomney expressed his interest and was invited to Chelsea for an interview. "It was quite a challenging interview," he remembered. He met the Holmes family members at Weber's restaurant in Ann Arbor.

Tiny Holmes asked him what he could do for the company. "I told her I could help the company be profitable," Tomney said. "We already make enough money," she told him. "Then I added that the job of a chief financial officer was to help position the company so that it would continue to be competitive in the future, by paying attention to costs and vendor relationships, making changes that might be necessary, and helping move the company in the direction the family wished to move it."

He got the job. Years after Tomney arrived, he was told that when the board of directors had suggested to Howard that the company could use a chief financial officer, Howard had pounded the table and asked, "What will he do all day?"

"I'd like Howard to know that I never found a dearth of things to keep me busy!" recalled Tomney with a smile.

Shortly before Tomney arrived, Chelsea Milling acquired its first computer system, but there were problems balancing the books. That was the first job on Tomney's checklist. Then he and Howdy analyzed the staggering overtime premiums, which amounted to nearly $1 million a year. "Change started with the concept of 'Jiffyville' and the train leaving the station," he said, adding, "Chelsea Milling continues to change." By the time Tomney retired in the summer of 2003, he had investigated every nook and cranny of the company's financial picture, from insurance to employee benefits, vendor costs, capital outlay, and sales budgets.

Bernie Schipper was officially retired when Howdy talked him into joining JIFFY. In 1991, John Rutherford attended the party for Schipper's retirement from his job as Meijer's director of grocery buying. One of Meijer's buyers told Rutherford that Schipper probably would not stay in retirement and suggested that someone from JIFFY call on him. Rutherford passed the message on to Howdy and Schipper was hired on a part-time basis to manage Chelsea Milling's seventy-three food brokers, a job left vacant when Bob Rutherford retired in 1990.

"It was quite a job," Schipper said. He remembered spending two and a half years trying to "level the playing field for Chelsea Milling, making sure we had control of our business, because the company was being managed by the brokers rather than vice-versa."

In time, Schipper was named director of sales and put in charge of the company's direct sales force as well as the brokers. Chelsea Milling added four regional sales managers and reorganized internal reports, controls, and accountability standards.

While Chelsea Milling was fine-tuning internal changes, the industry itself was changing dramatically. Stores were consolidating and centralizing—"which means that the customer can leverage more

BERNIE SCHIPPER SHARING A JOKE WITH HOWDY.

power over the manufacturer," said Schipper, explaining that nowadays, thirty customers are responsible for 80 percent of the JIFFY business. Kroger bought six or seven major retailers, Safeway bought five or six, and six monster companies emerged. Meanwhile, food brokers were also consolidating. All of these changes meant that manufacturers had to change their approach to sales.

Chelsea Milling had some important strengths that made the changes more manageable, according to Schipper. "We can make decisions quickly and change direction immediately if we have to," he said. "On the other hand, there are some things we couldn't change because of sixty-plus years of company culture." In 1977, for example, government-instituted wage and price freezes caused manufacturers to raise product costs ridiculously, to protect themselves against the possibility of future price freezes. While JIFFY's competitors increased promotional allowances to customers and raised advertising budgets for couponing and media support, Chelsea Milling, true to its heritage, refused to follow their lead. "A case of JIFFY product might sell for nine dollars, while a competitor's case would be sixteen dollars. The seven dollar difference reflected the inflated cost protection against possible price freezes," Schipper explained. Again, the company's choice to not raise prices to protect itself resulted in its ability to weather the change in the market by maintaining its market share.

The future offers even more challenges. Fewer people are baking and cooking from scratch; more are buying prepared or refrigerated foods. Americans are eating out more often. Howdy described this as "a generation of quick fix"—and all this makes selling prepared mixes a greater challenge. "In a business world which has a lack of integrity and definitely a lack of trust, Chelsea Milling Company has remained true to its values, while making significant and positive changes and improvements," said Schipper. "What Howdy did was to retain the culture, but accelerate change in the company to bring it up to speed in terms of facilities, systems, and people. That enhanced the company. It has been consistent in delivering quality and value to the customer. The company is respected for its honesty and integrity. People know that if they call with a problem, it'll be handled, not pushed under the rug. What Chelsea Milling was sixty years ago, it still is today."

Schipper continues to work at Chelsea Milling as a consultant.

D ressed in a blue uniform and white hair net, packaging line worker Anna Louise Knickerbocker was oblivious to the constant *whirr-whirr* and *clunk-clank* of the packaging machinery all around her. In an interview in the early 2000s, she introduced herself by saying, "I'm the top seniority person in the whole plant." Howard's pet name for her was Lukie, and "Old Dud just called me Luke," she recalled with a smile, taking a well-deserved break in the middle of the morning. "I came here in 1953 from Salyersville, Kentucky, the same town that Luke Collinsworth came from, when I was Anna Louise Salyer, a sixteen-year-old girl." She intended to work during the summer then go to college. She went home for a few months, returned to the mill on

July 25, 1954, and never left— except for six weeks of maternity leave for each of her five children.

Knickerbocker was proud of the fact that in almost fifty years she had never missed a day's work due to weather. For most of the years she worked at the mill, she walked the six or seven minutes to work every day and scheduled her shifts so she could be home by the time her children returned from school.

In 1977, Howard hired her husband as a machinist; he worked at the plant for nearly twenty years. "There was a time when people told me I was crazy to stay here, because the auto industry was going great guns and paying so well," said Knickerbocker. "My sister worked at Chrysler;

SEALED PACKAGES OF JIFFY SPEED THEIR WAY TO THE BALER TO BE CASED FOR SHIPPING. FROM THE TIME THE WHEAT ARRIVES AT THE MILL, THE MIX IS NEVER TOUCHED BY HUMAN HANDS—ALL THE WAY TO ITS FINAL SHIPPING CASE.

she's at JIFFY now. When her plant was moved to Alabama, she had two small sons and didn't want to move. I went to Howard and he told me, 'Tell her not to go.' That's how she got her job here. My brother went into management in Ann Arbor, but he's third shift leader for packaging at JIFFY now. I have a lot of family working here. That's true for most people. Family is still an important consideration here."

The company focus on quality, not quantity, has made her proud, said Knickerbocker. "We always strive to meet or exceed expectations, and we go the extra mile if possible. Our success is documented. And it's appreciated." Often, after the annual audit by the American Institute of Baking, the company will as a reward treat employees to a hot dog roast or something else fun, she said, explaining, "It's not the expense of a hot dog lunch that is important; it's the idea that Howdy appreciates what we do. Now, that matters."

As close as she was to Howard, Knickerbocker became intrigued by the changes that Howdy proposed when he arrived. "Those of us who worked here in the late 1960s and 1970s had followed Howdy's racing career," Knickerbocker said. Howdy came with a different experience in the business world, a different perspective, and a realization that one person just can't do everything. I don't think it's realistic to expect someone to come in and step right into the shoes his father wore." Howdy seemed willing to do the things that she thought needed to be done. "A lot of people don't realize that you have to change with the times," she said. "We needed some key people to keep the business competitive, and Howdy proceeded to hire them. He told me that his goal was to have the place under professional team management within ten years of his coming—and he managed to do that. After all, it's to our best interest to keep this business competitive!"

Knickerbocker put away her coffee cup and prepared to return to her shift. "I've always enjoyed working with the girls in packaging. I still do," she said. "That's why I'm still here. When people ask me about retirement plans, I just smile and say, 'It's awfully hard to give up this gravy job.'"

Knickerbocker retired in 2005, after more than fifty years at the mill.

D r. Everett Everson, retired director of the Wheat Research Program at MSU and former member of the Chelsea Milling Company's board of directors, was a familiar and welcome face around the Chelsea plant during the week when the board met. "It's like coming home for me," Everson said in an interview before he left the board. "I feel like a part of the family." He made the rounds of the mill every month, greeting millers and line operators by name and noticing any changes in people or machinery. "I was the first outsider invited onto the board of directors here, in 1991," he recalled, "but my friendship with the family goes back to 1955."

In that year, Michigan still had operating mills in the cities of Frankenmuth, Augusta, Lowell, Ionia, Portland, Grand Rapids, Dowagiac, Hillsdale, Monroe, Quincy, Mount Pleasant, and Detroit, as well as in Chelsea and a few other locations. Up until that time, Michigan's farmers were planting and harvesting New York varieties of wheat called Yorkwin and Genesee. "The farmers wanted varieties with better yield, and the mills wanted varieties with excellent quality," Everson said. Howard and Dudley were eager to support efforts to develop wheat varieties designed specially for Michigan's soil and climate, and promised that the industry would give financial support to the creation of a new wheat-breeding position at Michigan State.

A wheat breeder with degrees in agronomy and plant genetics, Everson was working at Washington State University at the time he was recruited by MSU. "I wasn't interested in changing jobs until I met Howard and Dudley Holmes—they were charming. It was an easy sell after that meeting," he remembered. Howard extolled the outstanding

DR. EVERETT EVERSON (CENTER) JOINED MICHIGAN STATE UNIVERSITY AS ITS WHEAT BREEDER AFTER MEETING DUDLEY (LEFT) AND HOWARD IN 1955.

virtues of the state of Michigan, and together both brothers talked about the state's milling industry and its need for new wheat varieties. Shortly afterward, Everson joined the MSU Department of Crop and Soil Sciences as its wheat breeder.

Six years after his project began, the first variety of homegrown, homebred wheat was released under the name Ionia. Everson's department named the wheat varieties after the sites of old gristmills in Michigan. Because the varieties of plant diseases and insects can mutate (which means they can circumvent the resistance built into wheat varieties), research must go on continuously. Under Everson's direction, his department released a new variety of wheat every five or six years. Tecumseh, Augusta, Frankenmuth, Chelsea, and a red wheat named

HOWDY WITH ARLENE HONBAUM (LEFT) AND DELORES FOUTY.

Hillsdale were all released before he retired from MSU in 1989.

When the wheat-breeding project began, the statewide yield averaged twenty-six bushels of wheat per acre; when Everson retired, farmers were producing sixty-five bushels per acre. "Part of the increase in yield was due to the increased use of nitrogen fertilizer and the wheat plant's ability to respond to it," Everson explained. Unfortunately for farmers, as the wheat yield increased, the price per bushel declined. So did the acreage under cultivation. "The industry needed about twenty-five million bushels at the time, and we were just on the fringe of producing enough for the industry in Michigan and for companies like General Mills and Pillsbury, who shipped wheat to mills outside of Michigan," he said. To help with the demand, Ontario farmers started planting Michigan's varieties and increased their own wheat production. They are now major suppliers to Michigan's mills.

Michigan soft wheat is valuable not only to bakers, but also to the cereal industry. Soft wheat offers excellent quality for baking cookies, cakes, biscuits, and crackers, and for making ice cream. However, because the protein content of soft wheat is low, its flour isn't ideal for working with yeast. Bran is an important by-product of milling and an important ingredient in many breakfast cereals. "The companies that make bran products prefer white bran (the same type produced as a JIFFY by-product) because red bran has a slight astringency," said Everson.

Delores Fouty, from accounts payable, joined the company in 1957 at the age of seventeen. She was still in high school. Her father, a longtime Chelsea Milling employee, had just passed away, and Howard Holmes guessed that times might be difficult for her family. "Chelsea Milling really was like a family to me," she recalled during a lunch-hour interview on a day in the early 2000s. "My father wasn't the only one who had worked here. So did my mother's cousin and his wife [Veryl and Bernadine Hafley], my uncle, cousins, nephews, a brother-in-law, and his wife."

Like many young people, Fouty started as a "gofer" in the office,

DELORES FOUTY IN A 1958 ADVERTISEMENT FOR THE NATIONAL CASH REGISTER COMPANY. FOUTY SAW GENERATIONS OF TECHNOLOGY COME AND GO DURING HER FORTY-SEVEN YEARS WITH CHELSEA MILLING.

answering the telephone, running errands, and mailing invoices. At that time, fifteen people worked in a tiny office next to the storage tanks. Not only was space tight, so were the bonds among the office staff. "Everyone was very friendly and included you in on everything that was going on in their lives," she said. When she graduated from high school, Howard came to her celebration. When her first husband died, Howard came to comfort her. "I loved Howard," she said simply.

When Fouty started working, Mabel Holmes was still coming to work, driven to Chelsea Milling by her chauffeur. Changes came so gradually that often they seemed to go unnoticed. Mabel retired. Farmers stopped bringing in their own wheat. A new office building offered more space. Fouty took on more responsibilities, first billing, and then payables. Procedures became more formalized. The number of employees multiplied more than eight times. She gave up her old IBM machine and learned to operate a computer. She used to give plant tours, but now has no time for tours. "I saw Ron Borders paralyzed here and I saw the explosion that injured Dale Horning," she recalled. "I watched Howard grow old, and we all wondered how long he would be able to go on. I watched Howdy grow up and become CEO.

"This place long ago became a part of me."

Delores Fouty retired in 2004, after almost fifty years at the mill.

"Teamwork is my strength. I love to create, to bring order," said human relations director Pat McGraw in a 2002 interview (McGraw retired that year after seven years at the mill). The human resources field has changed dramatically and so has its impact on Chelsea Milling employees. In response to a series of employee surveys, Chelsea Milling began to offer a long list of benefits: improved health care, cash to waive (money back if you don't need medical insurance), health care reimbursement accounts, AFLAC supplemental coverage, and a 401(k) plan, as well as improvements to the dental plan, vision plan, prescription drug plan, and profit sharing. Chelsea Milling has become a drug-free, alcohol-free workplace with a strong continuing education program.

McGraw described the company's human resources policy as "firm but fair. Chelsea Milling has taken a strong stand on attendance and

confidentiality," she said. "This is a small town and the company has a small-town approach to many things, but this company wants to offer its employees the security of knowing their affairs are strictly confidential. We've also educated our employees about what is acceptable behavior in the workplace. What was regarded as okay behavior six or seven years ago is not necessarily acceptable in today's world. The net effect is that people now know what to expect and what is expected of them."

The quality of life at the company has risen in the past decade, she said. In 2002, Chelsea Milling's on-site accident rate was nearly half the national average for manufacturers of prepared mixes. Every year, the company strives to reduce those numbers even more. Employee turnover is relatively low, and mostly due to retirements. "Expectations are now made very clear to employees from the day they join the company," said McGraw.

From the standpoint of business integrity, people couldn't ask for a better place to work, McGraw said. "Some of my peers are dealing with ethical issues in their jobs. I never had to worry about that. I never had to worry about being turned down on something when it was the right thing to do. Howard, Howdy, Bill, and Dudley all have had a strong commitment to the well-being of the organization and the employees. Howdy believes that this company is his mission in life, and I think he lives his life following that sense of mission."

----------- JIFFY -----------

THE RIGHT INGREDIENTS
A Century of Family Tradition Continues

HOWARD SAMUEL HOLMES AND MABEL (CENTER) WITH FRIENDS.

M embers of the Holmes-Peters-White family have been millers and mill owners somewhere in the Midwest since the early 1800s, and mill owners in Chelsea since 1896. Long before arriving in Chelsea, they learned that milling is much more than a business—it is truly the heart and lifeblood of a town. This deep connection to community has clearly been passed down from generation to generation of the Holmes family, and the result is a business with a conscience and heart that are rarely found in today's fast-paced, profit-driven, competitive society.

It's natural to want the good guys to win, but too often a company's good intentions get lost in the battle for survival or the desire for a competitive edge. In the end, many who succeed in business have sacrificed at least some of their core values to get there. In stark contrast, the Chelsea Milling Company has managed to hold on to its values and principles for more than a century, while continuing to compete successfully with industry giants many times its size. What's perhaps even more impressive is the way the company has quietly but effectively prospered over the years without tooting its own horn in massive marketing campaigns or razzle-dazzle packaging. *Fortune* magazine perhaps said it best in its 2001 article:

> *You're in the supermarket, with the usual barrage of bells and whistles competing for your attention. New-and-improved this, flavor-blasted that. It's all so assaulting, it becomes a blur. Then you turn your shopping cart in the baking aisle, and there they are—those simple little blue and white boxes, so perfectly designed that they resemble totems or trinkets. No screaming typography, no sensory overload. They seem not so much retro or anachronistic as timeless. Even the name feels iconic: JIFFY.*

Today, a drive down the two-lane street of downtown Chelsea past the white JIFFY towers induces a sense of wonderment. The town itself is like something one might see displayed neatly on a miniature train table. Chelsea's nineteenth-century Italianate storefronts lead down to a statuesque brick tower whose clock has chimed the hour since 1907. Directly across the street, multiple train tracks run through the JIFFY complex past a serene graveyard where three generations of the Holmes family now rest under a modest stone monument.

The side streets of Chelsea are filled with meticulously maintained historic homes, their yards lush with old-fashioned gardens and picket fences. But Chelsea is not lost in a time warp, as the growing number of unique and fashionable shops that line Main Street attest. Its old-town charm makes it appealing to residents and visitors alike. And visible from every corner of downtown, JIFFY's stately towers gaze over the city like some beneficent giant. One can't help but wonder if the Chelsea Milling Company is the reason that the town has maintained its old-fashioned values, or if it's the other way around. In any case, the city and the mill feel as right together as whipped butter and corn muffins.

Everything about the mill feels clean and wholesome. If you didn't know better, you'd think that this wholesome image was the invention of some clever advertising agency. But that's where real and imaginary part company—there are some things that cannot be fabricated. "A walk through the factory floor, where scores of little blue boxes make their way like tin soldiers through filling, weighing, sealing, and packaging stations, reveals a decidedly chipper workplace, with friendly employees who seem to be genuinely enjoying their jobs," wrote the *Fortune* reporter. "They greet [Howdy] Holmes warmly, he appears to know virtually all of them by name, and none of it feels phony."

Through the years, more than one writer has whimsically referred to the Chelsea Milling Company as the "little giant" of the dry-mix industry. Since 1907, when Harmon S. Holmes acquired Chelsea's mill, the Holmes family and their employees have held their own against behemoth competitors such as General Mills and Pillsbury. The market research firm Information Resources reported in November 2006 that JIFFY was the leader in the $170 million-a-year muffin-mix category, with 29 percent of the revenue in this market, and an amazing 57 percent of total unit sales.

How has Chelsea Milling stood head and shoulders above its competitors for more than seventy years? The accomplishments make an impressive list. In addition to initiating the nation's prepared-mix industry, Chelsea Milling was the first company in the world to have a complete conveyance system, one that originally totaled over twenty miles in length. Chelsea Milling Company was the first American firm to introduce computer-controlled packaging and transport lines. Howard S. Holmes also installed electronically controlled equipment with a sorting system that segregated products, and an electronic memory circuit that could precisely fill orders. "This was revolutionary for its time," said Howard's friend and colleague in the milling industry Donald M. Mennel. "The trade magazines all wrote articles about it. Howard's warehouse system was the forerunner of today's computerized warehouse."

Although Chelsea Milling Company deserves accolades for its

many technological and innovative advancements, perhaps its greatest accomplishment is holding true to values that are so old-fashioned that the business world now views them as revolutionary. The company simply does not play by the same rules followed by most of corporate America. No one has ever seen—nor will ever see, according to Howdy Holmes—television commercials, print advertising, coupons, or any billboards for JIFFY products beyond the blue and white sides of semi-trucks seen barreling to stores and institutions around the nation. It's a nearly unthinkable strategy in the modern, media-saturated environment, and Holmes readily admits it probably wouldn't work for a brand being launched today. But as *Fortune* observed, "JIFFY has built up so many generations' worth of goodwill in American kitchens that it can get away with it."

Chelsea Milling's history of goodwill has been well documented. It extends back to World War I, when millers worked around the clock to feed the allied armies; to the 1920s, when Harmon and Howard S. Holmes hired local men and boys who needed to support families; and through the darkest days of the Depression, when Howard Holmes (and later his twin sons) resolved never to close the mill or lay off a single employee. The sacrifices extended to the World War II years, when Dudley left to fight in the Pacific and the second Howard Holmes remained at home to help fight hunger throughout the war-torn world. "Throughout the twentieth century, Chelsea Milling employees knew that they could count on the family to do the right thing for the company, for their employees, for their community, and their nation," said Lynwood Noah. "You can't ask any more of a business or a businessperson than that. Very, very few businesses in the world today can boast of the accomplishments and contributions that Chelsea Milling has quietly achieved through the years."

Despite the long shadow that the mill throws across the dry-mix industry, its hometown of Chelsea, and the nation, the Chelsea Milling Company continues today to remain a small-town, family-run, privately held company with values that were established more than a century ago. When Howdy Holmes says, "I feel as though I'm standing on the shoulders of my father and my grandfather and his father before him," he means it. But the Chelsea Milling Company represents much more than the success of one particular family that has managed to hold on to one particular business. It stands as a testament to the success of a set of core values established generations ago. Howdy Holmes once explained to a reporter, "Some of the old ways we're talking about aren't the old ways of doing things but the old ways of thinking about things. Things like principles, integrity, honesty, loyalty. Those aren't going to change." The family tradition of values and principles extends to the company's employees, townspeople, and customers. This is a place where courage, compassion, and courtesy are as important as they were in the days when Harmon S. Holmes carried his gold-tipped walking stick to work every day.

One more ingredient not to be overlooked is the contribution of the Holmes women throughout the past 100 years. Certainly the credit for the conceptualization and development of JIFFY Mix rests squarely on the shoulders of 1920s housewife and mother Mabel Holmes. Mabel was thrown into the position of running a national corporation at a time when men dominated the business world. Most women of that time—if they held jobs at all—rarely occupied positions higher than clerical or factory level. Mabel's strength and competence in the business world undoubtedly affected her twin sons' attitudes toward women and their choice of wives. Dudley Sr. and Howard married women who served at their sides, but conceded the positions of status to their husbands. Women's contributions have always been revered throughout the mill. That's why so many wives worked there with their husbands.

The old saying "behind every successful man is a woman" might well have originated with the Holmes patriarchs. Howard's wife, Tiny, saw her job as "making Howard available." She understood that supporting him behind the scenes was the greatest service she could give to the company. At Tiny's funeral Howdy said he had waited to marry because he was "searching for someone like my mother, and when I finally found her, I married her." Howdy's wife, Carole, admits proudly to using Tiny Holmes as a model for her participation in the company. "My role has been simple—to encourage Howdy and give him a warm,

CHELSEA MILLING COMPANY CELEBRATED ITS 100TH ANNIVERSARY IN 2001. CONTRIBUTIONS WERE RECOGNIZED IN A FULL-PAGE ADVERTISEMENT IN THE *CHELSEA STANDARD* (RIGHT). A COPY OF THE COMMEMORATIVE WAS SEALED IN A PLASTIC TUBE FOR PRESERVATION AND SENT TO EACH EMPLOYEE'S HOME.

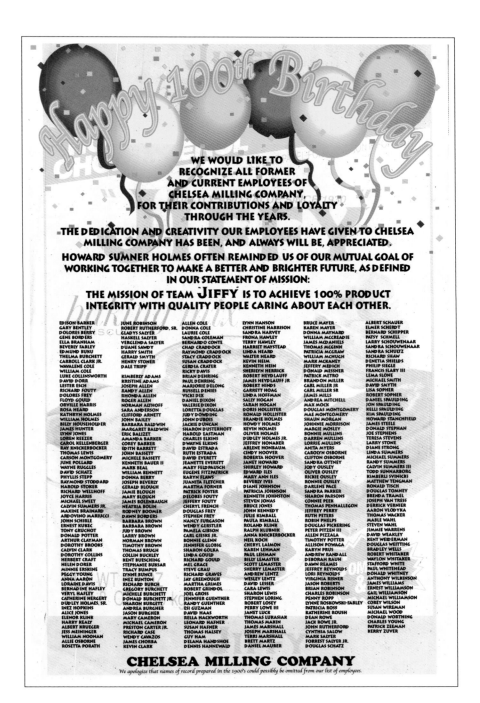

loving place to come home to," she said. "It sounds so simple to say that I've encouraged or supported him, but often there's a lot behind mere words. In order for Howdy to succeed, I've always felt that it's important for him to feel surrounded by love, a lot of positive thinking, and very little negativity." The support of a loving partner might well be the secret ingredient thrown into the mix that makes Chelsea Milling what it is today.

"Chelsea Milling has had a tremendous impact on the history, economy, and life of Michigan and the Midwest," said Chelsea attorney John Keusch. "If I had to speculate on the reasons for its success, ultimately I would say that the success is the direct result of the right people in the right place doing the right thing. For their employees. For their community. For their industry."

When Howdy was asked about his plans for the future of Chelsea Milling, he paused and gazed out his office window for several moments before answering. "I consider vision my most important job—and I do it with course and direction. What the future may hold for the industry, no one really knows, but people are going to continue to eat," Howdy said with a wink, "so we're not in that big of a rush.

"It takes more than a good product and a good sales niche to make a company work in the long run," Howdy continued. "It also takes good people. I think everyone has to figure out what they're good at, their strengths and weaknesses, and then fill in with the kind of people who can complement them. I've done that. I hope whoever comes next will do the same thing."

Where will Chelsea Milling Company take the industry and its family of employees in the next 100 years? One can only speculate—and hope that the tradition continues. It's a tradition that like the grain towers themselves stands tall and clean—against conventional wisdom about how to create a successful business. Chelsea Milling Company even challenges preconceptions about what constitutes real success. The kind of success enjoyed by Chelsea Milling is not easily measured by today's business standards, because the currency it generates is worth far more than any balance sheet can show. It's not hard to understand the pride and ownership that the town of Chelsea and the employees of the mill have felt and continue to feel for Chelsea Milling Company.

"JIFFY"

IN THEIR OWN WORDS

JIFFY Team Members
Share Their Memories
of Life and Times
at the Mill

These vignettes of life at the mill give a glimpse into employees' private lives and the general tone of the unique working environment at Chelsea Milling Company. Friends and employees, past and present, were eager to share their memories. Although every story is different, common themes arise of light-heartedness, kindnesses, and the feeling of being part of something larger than themselves. Each past or current employee was asked two questions to provide insight into why Chelsea Milling has flourished on so many levels. But some employees and friends wanted to share additional stories about the unusual events that occurred while they were working there and why they stayed.

Why do you think Chelsea Milling has survived and thrived for over 100 years?

When asked this question, the same three answers were expressed in many different ways: "We make a very good product at a very good price"—"We care about the company and the company cares about us"—"We feel part of a family that is bigger than any one of us."

Wayne Ruggles explained, "I think the attitude toward people, forged during the Depression, has made all the difference. In those days, most companies would work two days, then shut down for three weeks. This mill kept its people working throughout the darkest days of the Depression years, so employees would always have some money in their pockets. And just as the mill was loyal and dependable to them, they were loyal and dependable back."

Luke Collinsworth added, "They never tried to overdo things, to expand in a big way all at once. They kept us going steady, and they slowly grew the company. While they were doing that, they treated everyone as though we, too, were members of the family."

"Everyone worked together and helped each other out. Through hard times and easier times," observed Anna Louise Knickerbocker. She wondered whether modern-day employees could comprehend just how closely earlier generations of Chelsea Milling people felt linked to each other, to the mill owners, and to the success of the mill.

How does Chelsea Milling attract and keep their employees?

Employees and friends were asked to explain why so many people have remained throughout their professional lives and brought family members and friends to work at the mill as well.

"The Holmeses really care about their employees. They always have," Wayne Ruggles said. Once, when he was struggling with an income tax problem, he spoke to Howard, who immediately offered to loan him the money he needed. Another time, Howard helped Ruggles obtain a loan. "Howard was on the bank board," said Ruggles. "He made some calls and cleared away the bureaucratic debris."

When June Robinson's husband was diagnosed with cancer, the couple couldn't seem to locate a doctor for a second opinion. Howard made one phone call and they had an appointment.

Many years ago, Harry Kealy applied for a job at the newly opened Chrysler Proving Grounds and asked Howard for a recommendation. "We talked for an hour or more," recalled Kealy, "and I decided that I should stay where I was. I realized I'd never be able to find a job that suited me quite like this one."

The Holmes family has always believed in putting people first, retaining dignity and honor by providing unique and caring responses to situations that other companies might have turned their backs on.

Donna Lane's neighbor on North Main Street, Mr. Hansen, was head miller for many years. "I remember that the Holmes family had hired him when he was in his sixties—something you don't hear happening nowadays—and he worked there twenty years," she said.

Another miller contracted throat cancer. During that time Lane was working as a nurse in Ann Arbor, and she saw either Howard or Dudley visit the miller at the hospital every night. "Many doctors thought they were his sons," she remembered.

One of the company's firmest policies was to be generous privately. During a difficult time in Corky Palmer's life, Howard suddenly handed him a fifty-dollar bill. "I couldn't wait to get home and show my wife!" Palmer recalled some seventy years later. Other employees also remembered Howard's generosity in helping them get through tough financial times. Anna Louise Knickerbocker borrowed from Howard when she and her husband were buying their first house. "It was 1957, and we needed an additional $500 to buy a house in town that had no water or electricity," she said. "The old spinster schoolteacher who lived there was still using an outhouse in the backyard, if you can believe it. I remember we paid $4,500 for the house with an extra lot, and we needed a little more money to update the house. Howard helped us. He was generous to a fault with his loans."

Howard had a graceful way of being generous that allowed the recipient to retain a sense of dignity. After Luke and Sue Collinsworth married, they found a house for sale in Stockbridge, but needed an additional $1,000 to buy it. "I thought about asking Howard for help, but couldn't get up my courage," recalled Luke. One day Howard walked up to him and said, "I hear that you want to loan me some money." Luke's anxieties were relieved.

> *"The reason union efforts didn't succeed at Chelsea Milling is that Howard took care of his employees. They had no cause to need a union."*

The two men laughed and Howard loaned Luke the money he needed. "Howard let me keep my pride," Luke said many years later. "It takes a special person to carry things off that way. In fact, a lot of people borrowed money from him, and sometimes they would quit and not pay him back. I think Howard was stuck more times than we'll ever know."

When N. H. Miles's house burned down after he had worked for thirty-six-straight hours at the plant, Howard expressed his condolences, and then said to him, "This time of year our sales always slack off, so we have to lay some people off for a short while. I'm going to lay you off." That meant that N. H. could collect unemployment and have the time to clean up and rebuild. "We'll never forget how considerate he was," said Miles.

Howard was as generous to the community as he was to his employees. He often volunteered to help on the boards of organizations that benefited children: the Boy Scouts, the YMCA, local sports organizations, and St. Joseph Mercy Hospital. "No one will ever know how much he did for others," said June Robinson.

According to Anna Louise Knickerbocker, one of Howard's proudest moments was the day when he announced his profit-sharing plan. The employees had all been called to the Chelsea Congregational Church for the announcement. "In my case, the profit-sharing worked wonderfully," she said. "I'd just gotten married and we were just starting out. I'm a charter member of the plan and I've tried to put away as much as possible. That profit-sharing plan has made a huge difference in many people's lives." Cal Summers believed that the profit-sharing plan was the best thing Howard ever did for his employees. "Nobody asked for it. Howard just did it," Summers recalled. "Out of the blue, every once in awhile, he'd do something like that for his employees. One day he decided that our vacation would be raised to three weeks after eight years of working at the company. He came up with holiday pay, and he added new holidays to the list of paid vacation days every once in awhile."

"The reason union efforts didn't succeed at Chelsea Milling is that Howard took care of his employees. They had no cause to need a union," Lynwood Noah said. "He was a very smart administrator." The respect between employers and employees has always been a two-way street.

"If I were young again and starting my life all over, I'd want to go back and work for Chelsea Milling Company and stay there about a hundred years before retiring," said Dale Tripp. "You'll never find a better employer anywhere. Most of the young employees here probably don't know that, but when they get to my age, they will!"

JIFFY TEAM MEMBERS SHARE THEIR PERSONAL MEMORIES

William Cole had just graduated from high school in 1953 when he got a job at Chelsea Milling. Albert Doll hired him for $1.25 an hour—"which was good money then"—to work in the mixing department. He stayed there forty years, the last twenty of them as mixing department foreman. "Willis Heydlauff, Walt Zeeb, and August 'Curly' Dorer broke me in—we were the only ones in mixing in fifty-three," recalled Cole.

The mixing department generally ran two twelve-hour shifts, five and a half days a week, but when orders backed up, they worked seven days a week. When the plant shut down on Saturday mornings, the mixing crew would sweep, clean, blow the air vents, and fix the machines, getting them ready for Monday mornings. Like many others at the plant, Cole also did a variety of other jobs on overtime: packing flour and feed, helping with maintenance, pitching in with odd jobs. Many days, the crew worked sixteen hours, then reported back to work at 6 a.m. the next day. When he became mixing supervisor, he was on call twenty-four hours a day. "When I left in 1994, the company was running three shifts with close to sixty guys."

William Cole lives in Grass Lake.

A Kentucky native, Luke Collinsworth came to Michigan at the age of eighteen in 1958, "looking to better myself." His sister, Ann Borders, had worked in packaging, and she introduced him to plant supervisor Walter Scott, who hired Collinsworth temporarily to fix a shipment of cartons. "They needed someone to cross out one of the ingredients listed on each box," recalled Collinsworth, who retired in 1999 and still lives in Chelsea with his wife, Sue. "Walt told me that it would be a short-time job, but I guess they liked my work. I stayed for forty-three years."

His first year Collinsworth hauled stock and mixed glue; he was paid $1.25 an hour. Eventually, he became a mechanic. "In 1956, there were no automatic relays—everything was done manually," he said. "If something froze up or broke or got worn a little bit, we repaired it." Veryl Hafley had been his boss. When Hafley left, Collinsworth became supervisor.

Annual raises ranged between 10 and 25 cents an hour. Luke married two years after starting, and to make ends meet, he often worked an additional six or seven hours after his twelve-hour shift ended. He also worked on Saturdays and even Sundays.

Over the years, Collinsworth witnessed dramatic upgrades in packaging speed, thanks to the automatic balers Howard introduced. "When I started, we had no fancy equipment. The girls at the end of the line would grab boxes and fill a case. There was a glue pail by their side and they would glue the case, stack it on a skid, and men would load the cases and haul them away on dollies. Automation made a tremendous difference in how fast we could work and how much product we could produce."

Sue Collinsworth went to work at the mill when her children were babies. Her mother would baby-sit for her, so she could work the same shift as her husband, who was also her supervisor. "Although I'd had other jobs before, I stayed here because the job let me work around my children's schedules and because I liked the people," she said. "Chelsea Milling had more women than any other shop around, and they were friendly and easy to talk with. We had a great closeness. When you get to talk to ten or twenty women at one time during fifteen-minute breaks together, you get to know an awful lot about people." Sue Collinsworth stayed at the plant for twelve years.

Born in Dexter, Bob Devine used to haunt the train station when he was young, fascinated by the cars and the people who came and went. He came to the village of Chelsea in 1947 as a station agent for the railroad. Working very closely with Dudley, Howard, and Clarence Athanson, he stayed until the station closed in 1974.

Both Richard Fouty and his future wife, Dorothy, started working at Chelsea Milling in 1954. "We met here, so you could say that this is really a family-based business!" said Fouty, who retired in 1992. (Richard's sister-in-law Delores worked at the mill for almost fifty years.)

Fouty worked first in receiving, briefly in mixing, and finally returned to the dock. His team would have races to see who could load a box car or trailer faster. He worked ten or eleven hours a day, averaging fifty-five or sixty hours a week (but sometimes as many as ninety or 100 hours a week), for thirty-two years. "We all worked together. We all helped each other out," he said. When he worked nights stacking 100-pound bags of flour in box cars, one man would be positioned at the top of the chute; others would stand at the bottom and catch the bag on their shoulders, then walk to the box car and toss it up. "In the summer, when it was so hot and we were so sweaty, we'd have cake flour stuck all over our bodies. That job kept us in shape!" he said.

"What kept us going?" he asked rhetorically. "Howard always appreciated what we were doing. We knew there were times when he worked all night, too, and then went on the road selling. All the Holmes family ever asked of us was to do a fair day's work for a fair wage. The door to Howard's office was always open. That was true for

Dudley, too. And if anyone found themselves in hard times, all we had to do was ask and they would set us up. We'd pay them back so much a week from our paychecks."

Richard and Dorothy Fouty, who are no longer alive, were married for forty-eight years.

A Sylvan Township native, Veryl Hafley started working at Chelsea Milling as a boy in 1926. Then he attended Chelsea High School with Howard and Dudley. After serving in the military for four years, he returned to the mill and stayed until retirement in 1986. "Everyone worked together and helped each other out," Hafley remembered. He worked at Chelsea Milling his entire professional life and also met his wife Bernadine (pictured with him) working there.

Veryl Hafley died in February 2002, but Bernadine, who worked at the mill for more than forty-three years, still lives in Chelsea.

Joyce Harris left Kentucky searching for a better opportunity. She came to Chelsea in 1959 to visit relatives and decided to apply for a receptionist position at Chelsea Milling. She was hired and offered a good hourly wage. Harris was the only mother in her son's class to work outside the home. Her husband, Orville (shown in photo with Joyce), had found work at another business in Chelsea, but eventually he, too, went to work for the milling company, unloading raw materials.

At first, Harris was the entire customer-service department, responding to all customers' letters—the good as well as the bad. "Dudley would check my letters every day, to make sure I'd written them correctly," she recalled. "He and Howard both were very detail-oriented." Sixteen years after Harris arrived, Dudley trained her to become a materials purchaser. "That wasn't a complicated job, but it required a lot of attention to details," she said. "I called in all the orders, wrote the purchase orders, and sent confirmation to the customers." When Dudley Sr. retired, she worked for Dudley Jr. "He was nice to work for, very patient and kind. We got along well," she recalled.

"I stayed for forty years because I liked my job."

Joyce and Orville Harris are both retired from the mill and still live in Chelsea.

When Dale Horning was a boy, he would ride to Chelsea with his father to deliver wheat. "I would love to come to town and help unload the wheat," Horning remembered. "The farmers would be out here with their gallons of cider and beer. I remember when Corky Palmer took us in to see the baking mix line. I never thought I'd be working here someday!"

In 1964, Horning was hired in the mixing department. He worked

seven days a week, twelve hours a day, and sometimes would leave his twelve-hour shift there, then head to the warehouse for another eight hours of work. "I had been making $2.35 an hour working in Ann Arbor and started here at $1.90," he remembered. "The top wage was $2.35 once I got broken in, but I could work twenty more hours a week and take home $125. If you wanted to work overtime, the foreman would find work for you. Most people couldn't get by on sixty hours; they needed seventy.

"We had a nickname for everybody," Horning remembered. "We called my first boss 'Drano' because he could fix anything. William Cole's nickname was Boss Hog. Lester Esch used to call me Blondie. We had a lot of good times." One of his stickiest jobs involved working with sugar. "We'd use up to 750,000 pounds of sugar a week," Horning said. "The sugar came in rail cars, and occasionally, semi-trailers. In those days, the semis (which brought in 60,000 pounds) didn't have big enough blowers to blow the sugar up into the holding tank, so we'd either have to blow it into a rail car first and then up into the tank, or use a gravity box. That was a farm wagon with a roof and air vent, which we hooked up so the sugar could be blown in. Then I would take it out of the bottom." He once worked eight hours to unload a truck full of sugar on a rainy day. Long before they were done, the crew was covered in a sticky coating of sugar.

For ten years, Horning had been responsible for getting the sugar from the car to the holding tank. When the company stopped this practice, he bought the wagon and used it on his farm. Horning also remembered the almost asphyxiating flour dust that coated everything in the plant, and the tremendous physical labor required to prepare large quantities of mix. When he transferred to mixing after his 1981 accident, he worked the line producing doughnut mix. "Every batch had to be sampled," he said. "I would take the sample to the lab and I would have to eat a couple of doughnuts every time I went. One day I must have eaten about three-dozen doughnuts. I don't eat doughnuts anymore."

Dale Horning left the mill in 1984 and returned to farming. He and his wife live in Chelsea.

Harry Kealy grew up on a farm in Albion, Michigan. One day in 1945, while he was working for another dairy farm near Chelsea, he decided to knock on the door of Chelsea Milling. "I wanted to work part-time, to make a little extra cash," he recalled.

Albert Doll hired him to work temporarily in the warehouse, then in shipping, loading, and receiving. "This was during the war, when Dudley was still in the service and Howard was making all the decisions," Kealy said. "The mill ran all the time, day and night."

Company organization was loose, and employees often chose where they wanted to work. Kealy's jobs involved packed 100-pound bags of flour and 125-pound bags of doughnut mix. He also drove the company's 1941 stake truck to deliver flour and pick up supplies and parts. One night Albert Doll called a meeting and divided the plant crews into the wheat department, packaging department, and the flour mill. Jim Gaken became supervisor of the flour operations. Veryl Hafley went to packaging. Kealy took over shipping, warehouse, and receiving, and he stayed there until he retired in 1985— "although Harry never really retired," more than one employee has said.

Harry Kealy died in June 2003.

After the war, when supplies once again became available and competition was keen, Howard was personally handling all of Chelsea Milling's sales. But he soon realized that he could no longer sell to customers on the telephone. He needed sales help. He found Glenn Lehr.

Lehr had worked with General Mills in the 1930s and early 1940s, and then went into business for himself—but his timing was bad. "During the war, it was hard to get the equipment I needed," he explained. Still, Lehr managed to sell Kroger $250,000 worth of tote boxes, and Howard heard about it. He called Lehr and told him that he needed a good sales manager. Lehr met Howard on a rainy March day in a parking lot in Grand Rapids. They stood in the rain and discussed the needs at Chelsea Milling Company. Howard told Lehr that he could start the next day. The year was 1946.

Glenn Lehr, who is no longer alive, retired in 1970.

After earning his engineering degree, Jess Meininger worked in the phosphate industry until he was offered a job at Chelsea Milling in 1962. Mabel Holmes would often visit while he worked in the laboratory formulating mixes. "She was a very sharp lady, always interested in what I was doing," he said. "She knew what she wanted and how to communicate that. I had a lot of admiration for her."

Meininger helped formulate the blueberry muffin mix, with some help from Dudley Sr.'s friends. "Dudley always insisted on natural products," Meininger recalled. "Someone was making imitation blueberries in Chicago with natural products and they sent a sample to us. We tested them (they are actually flavored pieces of apple), and we used them in our muffins."

Jess Meininger retired in 1977; he died in July 2004 at age ninety-four.

"I was a city boy who always longed for life on the farm," said N. H. Miles. During high school, he lived with an aunt in Chelsea so he could take Chelsea's agriculture courses. "I started farming on a shoestring—make that half a shoestring—working for Art Grau south of town for ten cents an hour at the age of fourteen, doing a man's work," he said. "That was in 1941, just as the war was starting."

The Grau family raised wheat, which they sold to the Chelsea Milling Company. N. H. Miles worked as a sharecropper until 1949, when he started buying the ninety-seven-acre farm on a land contract. Because his farm was small, he rented additional land, including a plot at the Holmes's farm north of town. "Farmers lived by their wits and the seat of their pants in those days—they still do," said Miles. "Many of us sold our wheat to the highest bidder." One day at harvest time, Mabel Holmes stopped by to chat and asked where Miles was selling his wheat. He told her he planned to take the wheat to the Bridgewater mill because they were paying more. "I'll never forget that day," he said. "Mrs. Holmes left the field crying. I felt terrible! In ten minutes, Howard came to see me and he told me that the mill would match the price if I wanted to sell to him. I did."

That was his first meeting with Howard. "Ours was an association that I grew to appreciate very much," recalled Miles. From that day on, Miles brought his wheat to Chelsea and his children would beg to come, too, knowing that the JIFFY people would visit with the farmers waiting in line and offer cookies or cakes baked that day.

When milk prices dropped to five dollars per hundredweight in 1953, Miles knew that he could no longer make a living by farming. He was on his way to Jackson for a job when he stopped by the mill to collect for his wheat. Corky Palmer noticed that he was all dressed up, and asked, "Where are you going to preach?" When Miles told him he was off to accept a job, Howard found out about it and told him Chelsea Milling had work for him. He offered Miles a job as night supervisor in shipping and receiving, explaining, "We don't pay as much per hour as some, but we'll give you lots of hours. At the end of the year, your pay stub should look pretty good." Miles took the offer and worked twelve-hour shifts, then went home to farm. His crewmembers hoisted twenty tons per man during the twelve hours, lifting seventeen- to thirty-five-pound JIFFY boxes onto trucks or loading 100-pound bags of Chelsea Milling flour, bran, or middlings onto trucks or railroad cars.

"I was a working boss," he said. "And, like all farmers, I always tried to find the easiest way to do things." Trailers piled high with fifty-gallon drums of lard would back up to the dock. Miles and his crew would position a big truck tire behind the truck, and then unload the top tier of drums by dropping them onto the tire. The drums would bounce toward the wooden elevator in the old building. A man exactly positioned would spin the drums into the elevator. "We were creative in our approaches, so one or a few men could do the jobs of many," he recalled.

After two years at Chelsea Milling, Miles was offered an industrial engineering job with a firm in Adrian and went to Howard to ask for advice. Howard told him, "As a friend, I have to tell you that if the job sounds interesting, why don't you try it? You can always come back."

"That's the kind of man he was," recalled Miles. "I've worked several places in my career, but Howard Holmes was the best manager I ever worked for."

N. H. Miles worked at the mill for two years, from 1953 to 1955. He lives in Nevada.

Corwin "Corky" Palmer was working for a grain elevator in Grass Lake in 1943 when he was sent to Chelsea with a load of wheat and orders to pick up some bran. "I looked around and told Wirt Ives, 'This is quite an outfit!'" He also told him that he was looking for a job. The next thing he knew, Howard came out on the deck, introduced himself, and said, "Tell me when I can come up and see you and I will." Howard kept his promise, and Palmer started working at the mill in September 1943, for 60 cents an hour.

He worked seven days a week, starting out in the wheat department. "The dust got me down and I had to take allergy tests," he said. "I've still got a spot on my lung from that." He transferred to maintenance for two years, and then spent an additional twenty years in the packaging department.

Corky Palmer retired in 1977; he died in August 1998.

The Chelsea Milling Company was the first—and only—place June Floyd Robinson ever worked. In 1940, after a year of business training at Cleary College, she met Mabel Holmes in Fenn's Drugstore, and Mabel told her that the mill was looking for someone with business skills. Robinson walked down, talked to Howard, and was hired on the spot. "At that time, the office was located above the garage where the trucks were kept, over what is now the tour department," she said. "They usually started girls at twelve dollars a week, but because I had a year of college, I was offered fourteen dollars." Robinson filled in wherever she was needed.

"We all did everything we could to make this business successful," she said. "We worked long hours, even Saturday mornings, when Howard and Dudley would be loading feed into the box cars or dictating letters." Often after a week on the road, Howard would dictate eighty or more letters. On those Saturdays, Robinson bypassed her steno pad and typed the letters as Howard dictated them.

Everyone in the office—Howard and Dudley included—was in their twenties back then, and they had fun together. One day Dudley asked June to take dictation. As he sat back at his desk and began to talk, he took out a cigar and, intending to be funny, offered her one. To his great surprise (and probably hers), she accepted the cigar. "From that point on, whenever I took dictation from Dudley, we'd smoke cigars together," recalled Robinson. Howard and Dudley were responsible for giving nicknames to everyone who worked at the mill. Dudley called Robinson "Peach Cake," but that soon changed to "Peaches." When Robinson was expecting her first baby, Tiny and Nancy Holmes gave her a baby shower. Another, day Nancy invited Robinson to her home on East Middle Street, to teach her how to bathe a baby. "You'd never hear of that happening at any other company!" Robinson said with a smile.

June Robinson retired in 1984, and she and her husband, Horace, live in Grass Lake.

After serving with the army as a helicopter mechanic, Wayne Ruggles went back to school for additional training, only to discover that helicopter jobs were hard to come by. One day his wife's brother called and asked if he'd like to work at the mill. He was hired in 1961 as a mechanic, responsible for the machinery on production lines 1 through 10. His pay was $1.25 an hour, and Ruggles averaged sixty-five hours of work a week. "I made more by far in three months at the mill than if I'd worked nine months at any other job," he recalled. "I was tickled to have that overtime. I'd been married three and a half years, and we had some catching up to do financially." When another mechanic became sick, Ruggles and a third mechanic alternated eighteen-hour, then twelve-hour shifts without a day off for a month.

"The machinery was pretty much in a state that I would call virgin—the way it had come from the manufacturer," he said. "We had one machine on the biscuit line that had been sealing tops since nineteen-eighteen." One of his responsibilities was to remake parts as they wore out, keeping the old machines running. "It was a whole lot cheaper to make the parts than to order them," he said. "As a comparison, it cost $1,200 to make the parts locally, but $7,500 if we ordered them from the manufacturer."

Ruggles had been working in the plant for about four years when one day the mix started coming down from the chute like glue. His supervisor told him that Howard knew about the problem and that he was to "make do." "I marched into Howard's office and talked to him," recalled Ruggles. "It turns out he didn't know about the problem, and he was absolutely livid. He got on the phone, and before the day was done, that mix was good." A leak in the hopper had prevented the flour from going into the mix.

Howard encouraged Ruggles to switch to day shifts so that he could attend night school. Soon after, Wayne began freelancing around the plant, doing carpentry, electrical work, plumbing, welding, and making parts. Wayne was responsible for establishing the machine shop and tool room.

"I'm glad I worked there," said Ruggles. "I think I made some contributions in my time on the job."

Wayne Ruggles retired in 1997; he lives in Florida.

Bob Rutherford was hired in 1964 to sell JIFFY products throughout southeastern Michigan (everywhere except Detroit). After a year, he began supervising the food brokers, and several years later, the direct sales force. When Glenn Lehr retired in 1971, Rutherford succeeded him as national sales manager. "The decade between 1970 and 1980 was another dynamic growth period for Chelsea Milling," Rutherford recalled. "It's a tribute to Howard that the JIFFY name is what it is today," he said. "We never spent a huge amount in advertising. We had promotions, but no big ad campaigns. No coupons. Our selling point has always been quality and value. We had imitators coming out of the woodwork, but they aren't around today."

Together, Howard and Rutherford decided to build the sales

program around the corn muffin mix, which was (and still is) the best-selling packaged flour-mix item in the United States. "We told our sales people and brokers to take that product, put it on the shelf, gather the other JIFFY products around it, and use the corn muffin mix as an impetus to bring the consumer to all of our products," recalled Rutherford.

Chelsea Milling salesmen followed Glenn Lehr's lead and toured the country with packages of JIFFY products and packages from their competitors, then baked the mixes in front of clients. "We never deviated from the instructions on the package, so we were honest in our approach," Rutherford said. "The demonstrations were eye-opening to people. They couldn't imagine that we could sell products that good for a dime."

Few weeks went by without someone offering to buy Chelsea Milling, insiders knew, but Howard wouldn't even consider the offers. "He wanted to do things his way. I admire him for that," said Rutherford.

Rutherford retired in 1990 just as the fourth generation of the Holmes family was taking charge at Chelsea Milling. His son, John (shown in the photo with his father,) joined JIFFY's sales force in 1977 and still works at the mill today.

Bob Rutherford and his wife, Eleanor, live in Florida.

S andy Schultz came to Chelsea Milling in 1984, after working for the railroad industry—New York Central, Penn Central, and Conrail. Mill employee Tom Halsey told her that Howard's secretary, June Robinson, was retiring, so she filled out an application. "I worked my way into the Chelsea Milling Company the old-fashioned way, one step at a time," said Schultz. She started as a temporary employee, worked one week, and then got a request from Howard to work another week. In the third week, he told her that the job was hers if she wanted it. "I want it!" Schultz told him.

"Howard and I hit it off right away," recalled Schultz. "He was stately, elegant, very family-oriented in his approach to the people who worked here, and so comfortable with everybody around him. What impressed me was that he had such great knowledge and yet didn't mind teaching, training, and explaining. His patience seemed endless. I had a lot to learn. Also, I had never worked for a company where everyone was on a first-name basis, including the boss." Initially, she worked for Howard, Bob Rutherford (in charge of sales), and Clarence Athanson (in charge of traffic). As the company hired more people, they came under Schultz's administrative wing.

"Howard had such tight control over everything that happened here, and everything he did was in writing," said Schultz. "Now that he's gone and we've begun to clean out his office, I find stacks and stacks of his notes and memos. Those little notes are what helped him cross the bridge of memory adjustments so gracefully and adequately."

Schultz served as the company's bridge between the third and fourth generations of management. Although Howdy's return to the family business was a surprise to many people, Schultz quickly saw that Howdy felt it was something he had to do, for himself as well as for his father. As Howdy increasingly took on more responsibilities, Schultz worked with him on the administrative tasks and with Howard on everyday tasks. Howard always walked the plant on the first shift to see the employees, then he'd go out again so he could see the second-shift people, Schultz recalled. Too quickly, visits to the plant and a daily hot fudge sundae became the high points of his days. If Howard didn't appear in the plant for a few days, Schultz would get calls from both shifts asking where he was and how he was doing.

"When I think about Howard, which is often," said Schultz, "I think of his sense of humor and the ever-present twinkle in his eye. He so loved life."

Generations of Chelsea schoolboys were offered summer or part-time jobs at the mill to help them save for college or to assist their families through difficult times. Rolly Spaulding was one of those boys. In 1937 he went to work at the mill when he was still in high school. Sixty-one years later, he wrote to Dudley Holmes Jr. to share some memories about a silly prank he and his fellow shift members played on the women's shift while working at Chelsea Milling. His letter follows:

> *Hi, Dud!*
> *Rolly Spaulding here.*
>
> *Thought you would get a kick out of this—and you ought to know this ol' bit of history.*
> *Sixty-one years ago, I and my friends worked for Jiffy. . . . Myself, Fritz Zelser, Don Koebbe, Don Wheeler, Charley Winans, Tobie Hafley, Gene Martin, Jerry Dorer. . . . We were juniors in high school when Howard hired us, told us we could work 4 hours a day, but we were to set our own schedule. He didn't want our work time to interfere with sports—football, track, basketball & baseball. We were to set our own time around sports. So we became Jiffy workers. We needed it. Times were hard and I helped my family, my grandparents, with the food bill.*

Whatever, I had great fun working for Jiffy.

We were definitely the greatest bunch of workers that Jiffy ever had—or will have. We worked in the basement packing wheat farina for C. F. Smith Co. in small boxes and wheat hearts for Heywood Milling Co. in small sacks. Paul Belser would write on the blackboard in the basement what we were supposed to pack.

Prior to us, during the day, Florence Lurs and her workers packed the same thing and wrote their day's production on Paul's blackboard. They worked 8 hours. Me, being a smart ass at the time (I may or may not have outgrown that), thought it would be a great thing if us kids could pack more in our 4 hours than the women could in their 8! So . . . I organized it so we could do that.

The guys that weren't involved in sports got down early, didn't punch in, but started working. The rest of us got there as soon as we could. Didn't punch in, but worked and gave it hell. At the proper time, one of us punched us all in and we worked our tails off. Punched us out for the proper time and continued to work packing until we had packed more than the women—and wrote it on Paul's blackboard. Never before or after has Jiffy had such a batch of workers.

The women were mad. . . . After several weeks of us kids packing more in our four hours than the women did in their eight, Paul Belser showed up, said he knew what we were doing and the milling co. appreciated it, but we had to quit it, the women were mad.

We laughed, felt that we'd done a smart ass thing and made our point. Went back to doing just a good job that we were hired to do, although we did cheat a little and knock an hour or ? off the clock.

We did work hard and fast and earned money. We appreciated it and had fun and developed teamwork and working skills and the knowledge that work could be fun. Working at Jiffy taught me what work and earning a living were all about.

Thanks, Howard
Rolly Spaulding

When Chelsea Milling was preparing to launch its line of cake mixes and frostings in 1955, it began a hiring program. One of the first on board was Phyllis Stepp, who as a teenager had been a baby-sitter for Dudley Sr.'s children.

Shortly after the packaging department was automated, Stepp started working the afternoon shift. "The boxes kept coming down fast, and you had to be fast to keep up with them," she said. "I remember the first week I worked there—my hands were covered with blisters and paper cuts."

After a maternity leave, she returned to clean offices, then to help Dudley's wife, Nancy, supervise the test baking of products. Dudley would bring samples from the plant to his house, and Nancy and Stepp would start baking. Eventually Chelsea Milling built its own test kitchen, which became Stepp's headquarters, with Nancy coming to supervise. "It was definitely a family business," Stepp recalled. "Nancy was my first boss, then Dudley Sr., then Dudley Jr.

"Every three hours we would spot-check, looking for texture, size, color, taste—all the things that indicate a good cake. We tasted every product we baked," she said. Eventually, her crew baked and checked product every hour. If they detected a problem, the line was shut down immediately; the men would empty the fillers, clean the equipment, then mix a new batch. Within an hour, the line would be operational again.

Stepp saw mixes and ingredients evolve and change over the years; vegetable shortening replaced lard, and new spices were added to old recipes. Other companies and occasionally consumers looking to perfect their products or recipes would send samples of their products for Chelsea Milling to do comparison baking. "We had a lot to do. There were thirteen product lines and thirteen mixes to bake every hour,"

Stepp remembered. "I worked a ten-hour shift, though the other girls worked eight hours. As long as production was running, someone had to be in the kitchen. When production worked weekends, we did, too. On snowy days, someone would send a four-wheel drive to pick me up. I never missed a snow day. They always had to have someone in the kitchen, you see. I remember once, during a blizzard, I had to go home on a snowmobile."

When Phyllis Stepp retired in 1995, she had been with the company forty years. She lives in Jackson.

Cal Summers and his wife, Dorothy, worked together at Chelsea Milling. After his military duty in Germany ended in 1955, Summers became the shipping clerk, typing bills of lading and credit memos, while Virginia Wheeler did accounts receivable and payroll, and Viola Matthews supervised accounts payable. When Matthews left, Summers added accounts payable to his job.

He remembered many Friday nights when the office staff would stay at work until 10 or 11 p.m., trying to balance the books, even if they were only missing a penny. If they made even a tiny mistake in the statement, Howard would find it, they knew. "Howard would come in here and spend twelve hours straight on the books," said Summers.

In 1955, the office equipment at Chelsea Milling consisted of a big Western Union machine to send and receive wires. "It was a telegraph machine—with a regular keyboard, like a typewriter—several typewriters, ledger books, and a four-button phone with four lines," recalled Summers.

When Summers started, his pay was $275 a month. "In those days, the annual raise might be a nickel an hour, then it got up to a quarter," he remembered. He often moonlighted in the warehouse for additional pay. One year while working in the warehouse, he met Earl Marshall, a lanky southerner who told Summers he had been a pilot shot down on a deserted island during the war. Marshall could pick up a "pig"—two cases glued together for easier handling, totaling twenty-nine pounds— and he could tell by the feel whether it was on the light or heavy side. "He could spot a wrong product, and he kept track of the count as he loaded. He was quite a guy," recalled Summers admiringly.

During his forty-two years on the job, Summers supervised everything from personnel issues to payrolls to accounts receivable to accounts payable to insurance to computer operations to office managerial duties—and anything else in the office that needed doing. "In those days, people covered for each other," he recalled.

"Sometimes people just needed help, and everybody would help them," said Summers. He said he never forgot two things Howard told him when he arrived: "Young man, we do not solicit raises around here." and "Everyone has to work for a living, and I want to make it as enjoyable as possible for them."

Cal Summers retired in 1997; he and Dorothy live in Jackson and Florida.

Mike Sweet grew up on a farm north of Chelsea that had been in his family for 150 years. After high school, the army, and Korea, he returned home with only one idea on his mind: to not work on the family farm. "Jobs were hard to come by in 1962 and 1963. I went all over, looking," Sweet recalled. A friend told him about an opening at Chelsea Milling. He was hired on a temporary basis—"I think my selling point was that I could type." Back then, there were few titles and no job descriptions. Everything the office staff did was by hand—billing, check writing, and letter writing. The temporary job became permanent and Sweet was eventually put in charge of taking all orders.

Mike Sweet retired in 2000; he and his wife, Jan, live in Chelsea.

Dale Tripp worked many different jobs around Ann Arbor (for example, he was a chauffeur for Mabel Holmes), before coming to Chelsea Milling in 1953. "When I got here, it was like finding a home," he said. "There was never a dull minute." He stayed thirty-four years, retiring in 1987. Under the nickname "Compass Bumpass," he drove trucks delivering JIFFY throughout the Midwest. When he first arrived, there were ten drivers, ten tractors, and eighteen trailers.

"I started driving an old International tractor with a single-axle trailer, which was about twenty, maybe twenty-six feet long. I graduated up to a tandem trailer," recalled Tripp. He drove to Burlington, Iowa, Kansas City, Missouri, and everywhere in between. "Usually I would drive products to customers, then bring back waxed paper, flour, lard—sometimes five or six loads out of Chicago every week," Tripp said. "We'd bring sugar from Baltimore, soda from Arm & Hammer in Ohio, salt from St. Clair, waxed paper and little boxes from Rhinelander, Wisconsin. Every once in a while we'd load up on burlap bags in Cincinnati—we'd get 7,000 pounds at a time."

Dale Tripp lives in Ann Arbor.

CONTRIBUTORS

*We would like
to thank the following
individuals for their
contributions to
the book.*

Contributors in alphabetical order:

William Cole, *employed 1953-1992*

Luke Collinsworth, *employed 1956-1999*

Sue Collinsworth, *employed 1958-1973*

Bob Devine, *railroad station agent, Chelsea, New York Central 1947-1960, Penn Central 1960-1974*

Dr. Everett Everson, *MSU Professor Emeritus, Chelsea Milling Company Board of Directors*

Delores Fouty, *employed 1955-2004*

Richard Fouty, *employed 1954-1992*

Veryl Hafley, *employed 1937-1986*

Diane Holmes Hall, *family member*

Joyce Harris, *employed 1959-1999*

Carole Holmes, *family member*

Dudley Holmes Jr., *family member, Vice President 1969-2003*

Dudley Holmes Sr., *family member, Vice President 1936-1951 and 1954-1984*

Howdy Holmes, *President and CEO 1987-present*

Mary "Tiny" Holmes, *family member*

Dale Horning, *employed 1964-1984*

Bob Howe, *employed 1926-1946*

Roy Ives, *employed 1927-1930*

Harry Kealy, *employed 1945-1985*

Jack Kennedy, *employed 1995-present*

John Keusch, *family friend, community member*

Anna Louise Knickerbocker, *employed 1955-2005*

Wendell Kofler, *food broker, Greeson Company, Cincinnati, Ohio, 1947-present*

Richard Krafft, *owner, Star of the West Milling Company, Frankenmuth, and member, Chelsea Milling Company Board of Directors*

Donna Lane, *family friend, community member*

Glenn Lehr, *employed 1946-1970*

Pat McGraw, *employed 1995-2002*

Jess Meininger, *employed 1962-1977*

Donald M. Mennel, *owner, Mennel Milling Co., Fostoria, Ohio, family friend*

N. H. Miles, *employed 1953-1955*

Lynwood Noah, *family friend, community member*

Corwin A. "Corky" Palmer, *employed 1943-1977*

June Floyd Robinson, *employed 1940-1951 and 1963-1984*

Claude Sears Rogers, *lifelong family friend*

Wayne Ruggles, *employed 1961-1997*

Bob Rutherford, *employed 1964-1990*

Bernie Schipper, *employed 1991-present*

Sandy Schultz, *employed 1984-present*

George Staffan, *Staffan Funeral Home, family friend, community member*

Phyllis Stepp, *employed 1955-1995*

Cal Summers, *employed 1955-1997*

Mike Sweet, *employed 1963-2000*

Douglas Tomney, *employed 1993-2003*

Dale Tripp, *employed 1953-1987*

HOWARD SAMUEL HOLMES AND HIS WIFE, MABEL, IN 1912, WITH MABEL'S PARENTS,
ENOS K. WHITE AND HANNAH NICOL WHITE.

Acknowledgments and Index

Photo or graphic courtesy of:

Ann Arbor & Saline Historic Mills website– 15

Larry Chapman– 21, 22, 42

Chelsea Historical Society– 16, 28, 38, 41, 106

Chelsea Milling Company– 69

Chelsea Standard– 129

Chicago Tribune– 157

William Cole– 218

Luke Collinsworth– 219

Michael Fouty– 221 (top)

Bernadine Hafley– 221 (bottom)

Diane Hall– 51

Holmes family– 48, 49, 53–55, 61, 66, 76, 85, 87, 121, 126, 131, 135, 138, 148, 151, 152, 154, 156, 167, 206, 242, 244

Richard Krafft– 14

Pat McGraw– 205

National Cash Register Company– 203

Linda Penhallegon– 128

Ray Printing/CMC archives– 211

John Rutherford– 231

Cal Summers– 236

Mike Sweet– 88, 91, 192, 237

Washtenaw County Historical Society– 24

Lucille Williams– 45

Photographers

Joe Clayton– 71, 220, 224, 225 (top), 227, 235, 238

Jack Deo, Superior View– 36

Beverly Ives– 133 (center photo)

Cheryl Laimon– 188

Larime Photography– 174, 176, 180, 198

Katherine Larson– 168, back cover

Lynne Roskowski-Farley– 144, 147, 187, 228, 229

Andrew Sacks– 8

Sandy Schultz– 125, 132 (bottom photo), 133 (top photo), 145, 163, 191, 194, 199, 202, 223

J. Adrian Wylie– 178

Photo or graphic from:

Chelsea Milling Company (CMC) archives– 3, 10, 13, 19, 27, 31, 35, 37, 46, 47, 50, 52, 56–59, 63–65, 67, 70, 72–75, 79, 80, 83, 89, 90, 93–96, 98–100, 103, 104, 108, 109, 112, 114, 116–118, 120, 123, 132 (2 photos at top), 133 (bottom photo), 137, 140, 143, 160, 162, 164, 183, 184, 196, 201, 222, 225 (bottom photo), 232

Cleary Chronicle– 159

Headlight magazine, Chicago, Nov. 1895/CMC archives– 30, 34

Michigan History– 172

Past and Present in Washtenaw County, 1905– 44

HOWARD AND TINY HOLMES ON THEIR WEDDING DAY IN JUNE 1945. DUDLEY IS AT THE FAR RIGHT.

THE BOYS, DUDLEY (LEFT) AND HOWARD, WITH MABEL'S SISTER, ESTELLE B. WHITE.

Index

Marian High School
7225 Lahser Road, Bloomfield Hills, MI 48301

DATE DUE